NO-ONE MENTIONED BANDITS

To Carol
with best wishes

Joan K

NO-ONE MENTIONED BANDITS

Joan Khurody

© Joan Khurody, 2015

Published by Joan Khurody

A CIP catalogue record for this book is available from the British Library.

ISBN 978-0-9932558-0-9

Book layout and cover design by Clare Brayshaw

Background cover image © Karelnoppe | Dreamstime.com

Prepared and printed by:

York Publishing Services Ltd
64 Hallfield Road
Layerthorpe
York YO31 7ZQ

Tel: 01904 431213

Website: www.yps-publishing.co.uk

ONE

"Dilkhusha," said our driver with a flourish, pulling off the road and stopping in front of a large, decrepit building. "Name is meaning happy heart, Memsahib."

It might have been beautiful once when, with white arches and domes, it stood like a mini Islamic palace above wide green lawns. Now, with peeling paint, its entire upper storey cracked and crumbling, it sullenly fronted a scrubby expanse of weedy ground on which stood two broken-down cars in a state of disrepair that bordered on non-existence.

I had been married three days, two of them spent in dusty trains, travelling across India to this small northern town. My husband had already been here for two months, working as Production Manager in his company's newly built factory, six miles out in the countryside, while I had been staying with his parents in Bombay. Caught up in a demanding job, his first after graduation, he had snatched a mere five days to return home, marry me and bring me back with him. The on-site staff bungalow that he had been allocated was not ready as promised and a wing of the unappealing house in front of us was all he had been able to rent on a temporary basis. As we got out of the company car that had met us at the station and confronted our first home, I gave him speaking look. *My* heart was not happy.

"Come on, sweetheart." He unlocked an arched gate and took me into a walled courtyard, closed in on one long side by three lean-to outbuildings, on the other by a white wall set with deep windows and fronted by wide stone steps leading up to an imposing, pillared porch shading a heavy wooden door. Taking a breath and opening this, I entered a large, dim, sparsely furnished living-room and going through an inner door to the right, I found an equally spartan bedroom. Placed exactly in the centre of the floor were two charpoys. I was already familiar with these ubiquitous, naturally air-cooled beds, simple wooden frames strung with woven rope, but I had never expected to sleep on one. Between them was a round, carved table and behind them a huge and extremely ugly cupboard. A small window looking out onto the scrubland outside the courtyard gate was covered by a shabby batik curtain.

"Where's the bathroom? Over here?"

I went back through the living area and peered into a third room. "Is this it?"

There was no sign of a shower but in the far corner, formed by a raised tiled edging, was what seemed to be a shower tray with a low hole in the wall opening directly into the ground outside. Crossing over to examine this more closely, I glanced back over my shoulder and noticed behind the door, two low cupboards and a trestle table on which stood a paraffin stove and a small electric ring.

"Firdaus! Please don't tell me this is the kitchen."

I had difficulty with the rolled r in this beautiful name of his, normally using its short form 'Fi'. Hearing the full version, he knew that he was in trouble.

He took my hand. "It's not so bad. It will be like having a permanent picnic and I thought we could turn that ring upside down on two bricks and use it as a grill. We do have electricity."

"Great! Do we actually have a bathroom?"

"I'm afraid not. Didn't I say? Don't worry. I have made some arrangements outside. As a matter of fact we don't have running water either. It has to be brought in from that hand pump near the gate. I did tell you that it was all a bit makeshift but we'll only be here a very short time. I'm sure we'll manage."

We shared a long, silent stare. I knew, we both knew, that we had to manage not only these unsatisfactory lodgings but a viable life together. Too many people were sure that we would fail. Looking at him, I saw only the fellow student that I had fallen in love with. My parents had looked at him and seen a foreigner – worse than that – an Indian. His Parsi family, disappointed in their hopes of finding him a well-connected bride within their close community, had looked at the fiancée he had brought back from his time abroad and seen a very ordinary English girl. Each side had seen its child as the loser in this affair. They were all equally worried and upset. Not only was I marrying Fi but, by choosing to return to his country with him and live in a remote part of that country, I was also in a sense marrying India and they all believed that it was this that might defeat me.

Memory is a strange faculty and not necessarily a reliable witness to the past. It holds the oddest things in sharp focus, blurs others till they fade like old, sepia photographs and allows some things to die away completely. Why am I recalling mundane details like beds and bathrooms

3

and seemingly ignoring the fact that I am describing a controversial marriage making a determinedly brave start against an extraordinary background?

I think the truth is that it *was* these things that preoccupied us both for a time. We had been through bruising emotional turmoil in confronting our parents and friends with our relationship. Even now, in 2015, some families find inter-racial marriages difficult. In 1959, no-one approved of what we were doing and the strain of this had often led to stormy scenes between us, of both anger and passionate reconciliation. We were taking a breather. To focus on the demands of work and domesticity, even at this primitive level, was to move onto quieter, more solid ground.

That first day, though, the ground under me was far from solid. After viewing our unpromising rooms and Fi's 'outside arrangements', my legs felt disturbingly shaky. I went back into the kitchen and looked round rather wildly. We would need a meal, something to drink. What was I going to do?

"Jo darling, don't look like that." He came up behind me and stroked my back. "Listen. I've got a surprise for you. There's a Government Dairy Farm out on the road to the factory. It's managed by an Englishman. Well, an Anglo-Indian actually. He lives there with his wife and daughters in a huge bungalow and part of it is set aside for the use of visiting government officials. The Company has used its pull and arranged for us to stay there for a week. There's a proper bed and a real bathroom with hot water. And there are two old servants who will look after us. With operations in the factory just getting into full swing, I can't take any more days off but we'll be able to come here in the evenings and take our time to get things better organised and we can

4

go into to the bazaar to buy stores and groceries before we move in. The factory car is still outside and the luggage is still in the boot. We can lock up and go. I know that I should have told you about this before but I had some warped idea that it would be best if you saw this place without anything to cushion stark reality. Everything has been such a mad rush for me: getting to Bombay; the wedding and the family dramatics; organising our journey back; worrying about you and what you were coming to; work problems constantly weighing on me.......I haven't been thinking clearly. I have handled everything badly. I'm sorry."

He wasn't a talker and this spate of words showed just how nervous and edgy he actually was. I did feel a momentary flash of heat inside but I was too exhausted, physically and emotionally, for anger. After all that I had taken in my stride, it would be ridiculous to complain just as something pleasant was on offer and I was not a conscript in this venture but a volunteer. I reached up and stroked his cheek.

"It's alright. It's been a bit of a shock and I did lose my nerve for a moment. It's quite a relief to know that someone will be feeding us tonight. Isn't that crazy? We are supposed to be setting out on a great romantic adventure and all I can think about is food. Having someone to look after us sounds wonderful. Let's go."

It was already dusk as we drove northwards along a straight road that ran through flat fields stretching to the horizon on either side. This monotonous, almost featureless, landscape was broken only by the low, huddled roofs of occasional villages and a smoky haze, evocative of English bonfires, drifted across it, rising from the many cow-dung fires that village women were lighting as they began to prepare an evening meal.

After about five miles, we turned onto a side road that soon forked off in two directions. At the far end of the right-hand track we could see what seemed to be agricultural buildings but we went to the left between high, thorny hedges and emerged onto a wide circular sweep of gravel around a manicured lawn with a graceful silver-trunked palm growing in the centre of it. The bungalow that overlooked this imposing drive was a long, solid brick building with an elegant, pillared verandah running the full length of its facade. An exuberant bougainvillea climbed a central support and pots of scarlet geraniums stood like a guard of honour up the four steps leading to the main door.

Two elderly, white-clad servants emerged to welcome us with folded hands and soft voiced greetings. Then, suddenly strident, they chivvied two young boys in alarmingly stiff khaki shorts and shirts into dealing with our luggage, before taking us into the guest wing through a large, square hall that divided our rooms from the manager's quarters on the other side.

After thirty-six hours in the confined space of our two-berth sleeper, I greedily took possession of a huge bedroom and, as soon as our bags arrived, unzipped a holdall and unlocked a suitcase, spreading clothes over the high bed with its immaculate white cotton bedspread and setting toiletries on the polished, triple- mirrored dressing table.

Then I had a bath. During our long train journey I had showered in our tiny en-suite bathroom, swaying and fumbling with soap and shampoo, banging my arms on the walls, trying to ignore the gritty feel of the floor under my bare feet and finding it impossible to rinse properly with the meagre flow of lukewarm water from a partially clogged shower head. Now, I wallowed deep in hot water, in a large claw-foot bathtub, with white towels waiting on a mahogany towel rail beside me.

By this time it was totally dark outside and rather chilly. It was early December and until late February North India would enjoy a short winter with crisply invigorating, sunny days and cold nights. Fi, emerging after his bath in a white kurta and loose cotton trousers, had to put on a dark jacket and I wrapped a Kashmiri shawl around my shoulders. In the sitting room we found two leather chairs drawn up beside a large coal fire and the bearer, Taj Massi, had set out a tray of drinks for us on a side table. A little later he came to the dining room door to call us through for dinner and as we went in, I gasped with pleasure. An oval table was covered with a white cloth and four circles of marigold heads and loose petals had been placed along its centre, each with a tall candle inside it. There were two place settings at one end of the table and around these were more scattered marigold petals. The cutlery and glasses gleamed.

"Sahib, Memsahib, we are making a special dinner to honour your marriage."

"Taj Massi, shukria. Thank you. It's beautiful."

So few people had felt celebratory about our wedding that I had, almost without realising it, been left with a hard, sore knot inside me and this simple, open-hearted gesture moved me to tears. I was overwhelmed by the warmth and generosity of people who, with so much less than I had, could wholeheartedly delight in my happiness and their goodwill, their total lack of envy or malice was a healing antidote to all the unkindness that I had recently been exposed to.

The next morning, after breakfast, a factory jeep arrived to take Fi off to work. Picking out a rather tattered paperback from a shelf in the sitting room, I went out onto a back verandah and settled myself in one of several cane chairs there. I looked out across a garden shaded by unfamiliar trees. Immediately in front of me was another tall palm with a blue Morning Glory scrambling up it. The sun was bright but it was pleasantly cool and a soft breeze stirred my hair. There was a constant low hum of insects, the occasional call of a strange bird and the murmur of servants' voices from the house behind me but the non-stop, appalling din of India that had accompanied me for much of the time so far had suddenly subsided. I was at peace and, for once after so long, uncomplicatedly happy.

My solitude did not last. A small, plump woman with short, wild curls, wearing a cotton skirt and bright blouse, came out through the double doors of our sitting room.

"Hello. I'm Eva, the manager's wife. Mike, my husband, has told me all about you both. He said that I mustn't disturb you on your first evening but I couldn't wait to meet you today. I say that I couldn't wait but I have waited. I waited until I saw your husband driven off. Was that a factory jeep? You will have to get a car won't you, if you are to stay in town? Can I call you Joan? We don't need to be formal do we? Now, Joan, I want you to tell me all about England. I am English of course, but I've never been home. Taj Massi, who by the way is really happy to be looking after a memsahib, says that you will be alone all day. You must come and have lunch with us. You'll be glad of company and so will I. My three daughters have already come down from their boarding school in the hills for their winter holiday but they are staying with friends in Calcutta. They won't be home until Christmas."

I was rather stunned by this gush of information and questions but I had been away from home and among strangers long enough to have some sense of how meeting a compatriot in a place like this might lead to such pent up outpourings and, if Eva had never been to England, in me she clearly saw a compatriot.

From then on, most of my mornings were spent in her untidy living room, where her bearer waged an unwinnable war against the books, papers, knitting that she carelessly dropped as she moved from one activity to another. She talked endlessly and, though mildly curious about me and my marriage, asked avid questions about London which seemed to stand in for an entire country and which she apparently pictured as existing within a permanent, cold fog. I had lunch with her and her large, easy-going husband every day but, though generally tolerant of his somewhat scatty wife, he insisted that Fi and I should have our evenings to ourselves and, as she took a daily siesta, I also managed long, lazy afternoons out on the verandah with a book.

Our lodgings in town belonged to an India of harsh realities – the India that is both the exotic backdrop to most outsider experience of it and the daily ordeal of millions of its people. This place seemed to replicate a far more alluring version of the country – the India of the Raj. I didn't actually know if such houses were a legacy of British rule. The answers to many of the questions I asked in those first weeks were archived in deep recesses of my mind, lost to the moment, and even the future, in a flood of competing experiences. All I really knew was that despite its oriental setting, I felt an indefinable atmosphere of home here that gave solace to my already exiled heart. Dilkhusha loomed, however, unshaded in its wide stretch of scrubby, treeless land and, like a desert traveller, I would have to leave this oasis and face the challenge of it. Seeing me relax into the comforts and consolations of the guesthouse, Fi had abandoned the idea of evening expeditions into the bazaar and had managed to negotiate a full day off for our return so that all our shopping and any re-organisation of our rooms could be done then.

As we said our farewells and drove off, Mike and Eva waved goodbye from the verandah and Taj Massi and the other servants stood on the drive with folded hands. Eva had told Fi that on his way to work he must drop me off sometime to spend the day with her and had promised to visit me whenever she came into the bazaar.

I wasn't unsociable but I had always been reserved. I was a voracious reader, precociously academic, the first in my family to go to a grammar school and on to university. My father, though he had left school and started work at a young age, shared my love of books. My mother also enjoyed them but for her they were only a recreation while for me, and I think for him, they were a permissible escape into the more exciting, meaningful world that something in us craved. My mother was often impatient with us both and finding me reading when I should have been doing some household chore sometimes threatened to burn all the books in the house. She had been very much against my going to university and was only reluctantly persuaded by my father to allow me to go. This difference in tastes and outlook and a low-grade smouldering war of wills between my parents over my future had left me a little guarded and withdrawn. Though at school and college I had been on easy terms with everyone, I had no special friend and the general reaction to my news about Fi had somewhat darkened the way that I felt about everyone, even my contemporaries. Now, India was taking and shaking me, freeing me from my own inhibitions and the customary restraints of home. With limited amenities, entertainments and distractions, it would be essential to rely on others. As we reached the end of the farm track, I settled firmly in my seat and straightened my shoulders, glad to feel that whatever lay ahead of me, I was not completely friendless.

TWO

In the smoky dusk of our outward journey we had appeared to be travelling along a narrow, rural road. Now, in the fierce glare of morning, this felt like a terrifying highway. Our driver turned onto it, shooting out into a stream of traffic across the path of a huge, oncoming truck. Several of these rackety vehicles, mostly driven by large Sikhs in rainbow turbans, hurtled along the centre of the road in both directions, horns blaring, only swerving aside from each other at the last possible moment. Crashes looked unavoidable but were somehow always avoided. Single decker buses, so tightly packed that passengers spilled onto the steps, clinging grimly to any handhold they could find, also kept to the middle of the road and played chicken in this same unnerving fashion.

Apparently oblivious to all this crazy motor traffic, cyclists with packages tied to saddles and handlebars, pedestrians holding bundles on their heads with graceful, raised arms and a farmer shepherding a small flock of goats moved along at a more traditional pace.

Equally untroubled and slow were a variety of animal drawn carts. Many of these consisted of various-sized planked platforms slung between huge, wooden, steel-rimmed wheels that clattered along the hard road surface, adding to the general cacophony. There were bullock carts, buffalo carts, camel carts and horse drawn carts. The bullocks with their curved horns were really quite elegant and the buffaloes stolid and sturdy but the horses were all sharp-ribbed, pathetic creatures. One of these struggled past us on the other side of the road pulling a two-wheeled cart. Five men, clutching bundles and packages, huddled on its tiny platform, several legs dangling down over the high wheels, while the driver perched precariously on the front edge of it and held on to a shaft that rose almost vertically above the flanks of the horse. The whole ramshackle apparatus was tilted so far backwards that the horse seemed in danger of being lifted into the air. Soon after this we overtook a camel cart which, in keeping with the character of the animal, was a far statelier affair, four-wheeled, high-sided and deep, with a curved cloth-covered canopy shading its load and its driver. The camel plodded sedately along, its head high and its expression typically supercilious. Looking back, it seems incredible that for seven years, every time we went shopping, went to buy bread, eggs or tinned groceries, we braved this chaotic parade that so scared, fascinated and horrified me during our first perilous plunge into it.

Everything slowed down as we reached the outskirts of town and many drivers stopped off at a row of roadside shops and tea stalls. We threaded our way through a tangle of parked vehicles and carried on past a grubby cinema, a post office and a police station before driving round a large pond, bright with purple water plants, into 'our' road. Strictly speaking, this had to be classed as residential but there were no neat pavements or rows of pretty gardens. A narrow central strip of tarmac, covered in a layer of dust, disintegrated into sandy, pot-holed edges. On the left there were several large houses, partially concealed within walled compounds but on the right only a stretch of meagre, littered grass that ran along to a point where a sharp bend cut off any further view and where grass and weeds grew taller against the solid wall of some sort of institutional building.

Dilkhusha stood midway along this unkempt space, unique in being quite open and unprotected and we were lucky to have the privacy of our surprisingly well maintained courtyard. This was a symmetrical house and on the other side of its central block there was a second wing where an identical courtyard was a ruin, its walls caving in and its gate barely attached to its hinges.

Once again I stood in my unpromising kitchen. I looked round at the bleak, unpainted cement walls and the dingy, grey ceiling and floor and tried to think positively. As I have grown older a latent sergeant major always lurking in me has emerged but then I was so young, so untried and inexperienced that Fi, fresh from helping to organise the working of an entire factory and flushed with the newfound confidence this gave him, took charge.

"We'll make a list in each room of things that could improve it and then a second one of basic foodstuffs and stores. We'll go to the bazaar, get as much as we can and give ourselves the afternoon to sort it out. If we want more we can go shopping again in the evening."

So we wrote lists. Because we only expected to stay for four weeks, we simply put down essentials but they were still long lists. The ridiculous thing was that we already had household goods packed away in crates that we had brought from England. Fi's father had written to warn him that many foreign items, freely available throughout his boyhood, were becoming expensive and difficult to find in India. The Indian government was in the process of banning imports in order to encourage the start-up of local manufacturing and there would be an interim period of shortages. His mother had sent urgent messages asking him to bring back such unlikely things as O'Cedar polish and Brasso and telling me to bring a supply of cosmetics and sanitary towels as these too would be unavailable. Since I expected to be living in India for years this seemed impractical. How many trunk loads of these could I take?

I didn't take any. Nevertheless, quite a large number of packing cases had travelled with us by ship from Liverpool, in railway lift vans from Bombay and finally by truck from the local station to a storeroom in the factory where we had intended to keep them until moving into our bungalow. Fi had taken an optimistic view of our rooms but obviously seeing them through my eyes made him realise how bare and unliveable they were and looking anxiously at my somewhat grim expression, he quickly rethought this plan.

"I'll sort out the boxes tomorrow and get some of them sent here. We'll unpack crockery and cutlery, a few of your books, the record player and records. They'll make you more comfortable. But let's see what we can find in town. I've seen things like rugs which will make a lot of difference." He put his arms round me, looking both anxious and hopeful.

He had the use of the jeep until the next day when the driver, who had gone off to spend time with his family in town, would come to take him to work, so we climbed in and set off, bumping along the dusty road and rattling across a steep, hump-backed railway bridge that divided the comparatively peaceful administrative and residential areas from the noisy, crowded bazaar quarters of the town.

After three hours, we were weary and dishevelled but very pleased with ourselves. The back of the jeep was piled with buckets, an assortment of pots and pans, two simple cotton mattresses, two pillows, sheets, blankets, towels, colourful handloom bedcovers, four soft cotton rugs, several bright cushions and a bamboo bookshelf that had somehow found its way in among these. For once, Western efficiency and a driving sense of urgency had triumphed over the leisurely habits of the local tradesmen and we drove cheerfully back, only stopping at the bottom of the bridge to buy biscuits, chocolate, and fizzy drinks from a roadside kiosk manned by a large, dignified Sikh.

We stacked everything in a corner of the living room and went outside to sit on the porch steps for an impromptu picnic. We used brown paper bags from our shopping as plates and drank through the violently coloured straws that we had bought at the Sardar's stall. I leant contentedly against Fi's shoulder, buoyed up by the crisp air and the prospect of arranging our purchases. For a while we shelved all thoughts of difficulties and basked in a sunlit, drowsy contentment until we were roused by a knock on the gate and the sound of a sonorous voice.

"Mr Khurody. Mr Khurody."

"It's our landlord, Farid Khan," hissed Fi. "This could take some time. He's a great talker. Still, you must meet him."

He opened the gate and an imposing, barrel-chested man with a large, smooth face and greying hair, wearing a dark, embroidered waistcoat over a spotless white kurta and loose cotton trousers came over to me with his hands folded in greeting.

"Mrs Khurody! Welcome. Welcome. I regret not being here to greet you when you first arrived but I have been away, staying with my family for some days. I am delighted that your presence will grace my humble home for a while. Welcome. Welcome. But what is this?" He looked disdainfully at the remnants of our meal. "This will not do. Come with me. We will take tea together."

He ignored Fi's excuses. "No. I will accept no refusals. I am your host as well as your landlord. This is my duty."

We meekly followed him out of the courtyard, up the central steps to his door and into a large, square room that shared a wall with our own living space. We sat there on elaborately carved but very dusty chairs set out within a kind of clearing in the centre of piles of papers and stacks of boxes filled with what looked like spare machine parts.

"Please forgive this disorder but I have a number of projects in hand and need these items to be readily available and…....." he broke off to shout for his servant and we were soon served with a welcome cup of excellent tea and freshly fried savouries.

For a while we all ate in silence. We discovered that we were still hungry and Farid Khan clearly enjoyed his food as much as his own eloquence. Then, as he put down his cup and took a breath, about to launch into speech again, Fi stood up.

"That was delicious. Thank you. But if we are to be settled in by night we still have lots to do. I'm afraid we must go."

Farid Khan also rose, already unstoppably elaborating on the projects he had mentioned, talking loudly and gesticulating excitedly and next to this large, effusive man, Fi suddenly looked slender, serious and very young. They were in appearance and behaviour, symbols of two distinct traditions. Our landlord had a kind of faded Moghul grandeur and was a follower of a religion that has produced intricate and magnificent architecture and has ninety nine names for Allah. Fi had been shaped by the Zoroastrian religion of the Parsis, with its down-to-earth stress on the importance of good words, good thoughts and good deeds and belonged to a community that has produced a steel works and an airline. It was with this inherited common sense and a minimum number of words that he now firmly extricated us and led me away, leaving Farid Khan standing on his porch, still enlarging on a scheme to repair the wrecked cars in front of him.

Back in our kitchen, we re-checked our shopping list and headed into the bazaar again.

"There's a small shop at the top of the main street," Fi said, "where I've been for things like soap and toothpaste. It's called 'The Bombay General Store' which sounds grand but it's actually a bit ramshackle. Still it's quite well stocked as local shops go and we can get most of the things we need there."

It took time, patience and continual use of the horn to get through the throng of slow- moving shoppers in the narrow, crowded street while at the same time avoiding the goods spread out on the ground around roadside sellers on either side of us. The store, raised above street level and reached by three rickety wooden steps, was little more than a narrow passage with just enough space for us to stand between one wall and the counter. The shopkeeper, a middle aged Hindu with a perpetual smile, could not be rushed. He was friendly, talkative and intensely curious about us. Each time he turned from picking out an item from the shelves behind him, he leaned on the counter and asked further questions which we answered politely but rather evasively. So it was quite late as we drove back through the already familiar smoke scented dusk with bread, eggs, fruit and bags of tinned foods that we set down on the kitchen floor.

"Let's leave everything. I'll sort it all out tomorrow. I'll need something to do." I was suddenly tired.

Our evening meal was only slightly more elaborate than our earlier picnic. We ate scrambled eggs, not on toast, since we still had no plates, but between toast and used the empty bottles from lunchtime as glasses. Once again we sat on the step, with the light shining out from the room behind us. With no dishes to deal with, we stayed there for a long time, leaning against each other and saying little. I believe that Fi was afraid that talking might provoke me into raising uncomfortable truths and I was too overwhelmed by a kaleidoscopic medley of impressions to attempt to put them into words. The day had been pleasantly cool but it soon grew quite chilly. We were not exactly dirty but we were distinctly grubby. Fi went out to pump water and after heating some in one of the large pans we now owned, we managed sponge baths before braving our charpoys. The bed linen was stiff and had the slightly chemical smell of new cloth but we fell asleep surprisingly quickly, holding hands across the space between us.

THREE

The next morning, Fi was driven off to the factory and I stood in the gateway watching the jeep until it disappeared. As it turned onto the main road, he leaned out dangerously to give a last wave and I wanted to run after him shouting, "Come back. Come back. Don't leave me."

There was a clenching pain in my chest as if all the tears that I had never shed were tightly packed there, leaving me giddy with the urge to weep. I had often been lonely in the months before leaving England, isolated within the icy circle of disapproval, sometimes outspoken, sometimes implicit, that had united my family and friends. Nothing had ever been like this.

I went inside, locked the gate and sat on the step with my head in my hands, wondering how I would get through this day let alone the years ahead. Here I was, sitting in the middle of a remote little town that lay in the centre of a vast plain at the heart of a huge, unknown, perhaps unknowable country that until now had been nothing more to me than a triangle on a map. I had no idea what my life here would be like but it would be very different from any life that I had ever imagined for myself. Fi, a tenuous link with my previous life and the only guide to my new one, had just taken off into a separate life of his own that I would never fully share no matter how much he discussed it with me. He was at the start of his career. He had been given a good job and was under intense pressure to do well in it. He was by nature meticulous and attentive to detail and his rather distracted approach to our wedding and accommodation, made it clear that our personal affairs could not be his immediate priority. I was alone. It was up to me to make something satisfying for myself of this situation into which we had rather recklessly hurled ourselves. I didn't blame him for this. We had been unlucky as well as unblessed and since our arrival in India, nothing had gone according to plan.

We had met at University, a no-man's land between our disparate backgrounds, and in spite of our cultural divergence were immediately at ease with each other. We came from ostensibly happy families but in each there was a mildly dysfunctional element that had left both of us watchful and essentially lonely and we suddenly found ourselves sharing a more satisfying and comforting companionship than either of us had ever imagined possible. It was this as much as any deeper feeling, that had made us realise that we could not contemplate separation.

"Do I have go back?" Fi was thinking aloud. "What if I stayed on? No! I have a place and prospects in India. Here I'd only be an unwanted outsider. I have to go back. But how can I ask you to come with me, to leave everything and everyone you know, give up all you plan to do? Where we will be living, there will be no outlet for you, no real possibility of working. It won't even be like Bombay but much more limited in every way." He grasped my hand. "I can't go without you. Come with me and I will be everyone and everything to you."

Of course we knew that this was a romantic and unrealistic promise but the antagonism that we faced was like a cold blast driving us into a closed world where we huddled together for warmth, forced to the extreme of closing our eyes to problems and practicalities and concentrating only on our need to be together.

My family had been hard hit by our relationship and though it was only one element in their disapproval, there was no ambiguity about the racial undertone to their feelings. Fi was not allowed into our home.

"I won't have him here. I don't want him in my house," my mother said. "What on earth are you thinking of? You're supposed to be a clever girl."

She felt vindicated in her objections to my going to university. The journalistic career that I half hoped for had always seemed implausible to her and now like most girls, I was simply going to get married and probably, given who I was marrying, have endless children. My father, whose background had deprived him of chances that his abilities demanded, felt my rejection of opportunity keenly and feared that I would bitterly regret it. In the end, in the face of my determination, the best they could do was to insist that I should not get married before at least seeing India and giving myself a chance to change my mind.

Fi's family were widely travelled and used to a cosmopolitan group of friends. The Parsis were generally affluent and influential in Indian affairs and Bombay society and many of their young men were educated abroad. Mixed marriages, if rare, were not unknown to them and though it made them unhappy, ours was not the devastating blow to Fi's parents that it had been to mine. They might well have felt some of the disdain for me that my family felt entitled to in judging their son but there is no blinking the fact that simply being English, however undistinguished, still had some cachet and they had offered me hospitality and polite consideration.

Fi, one of a small group on a prestigious degree course in dairy science, had been marked out by his British employers for their projected Indian factory. He spent some time in their various facilities in England to gain practical experience and was contracted to be on site in the October following his graduation. Because of the quantity of our baggage, including my books and personal things, we had decided to travel by ship, taking everything with us but we had allowed for some time with his family before he had to start work and had sailed from Liverpool at the beginning of August.

There is something magical, even womblike, about being at sea, rocked by a rhythmic swaying that becomes a natural part of every movement and lulled by the subliminal heartbeat of a ship's engine. Every need is catered for within an ordered and contained world and yet, at its margins, stretches a dazzling expanse of emptiness and possibility. We had experienced a blissful sense of freedom, cut off from all those who had influence over us or ties with which to pull at us. Three weeks later we had come back to earth.

The ship had docked in Bombay in the early hours of the morning and I woke to a view of an ugly, concreted area filled with a huge crowd milling about and shouting incessantly. As soon as the gang plank was lowered, a group of people with armfuls of orange and white garlands rushed on board to greet us and as they converged on Fi, I stood there with the lost, sinking feeling that strikes a child separated from an adult in a crowd. I had slept badly and been unable to eat any breakfast. I was dizzy with mixed exhaustion, excitement and hunger. Fi introduced his father and his mother, a neat, spare woman with a strong, closed face who touched my cheek and forehead with cool, dry lips. He and I then spent three sweaty, noisy hours in the customs shed before setting off for his parents' flat. We had intended to stay with them for a month, exploring the city and meeting his relatives before getting married and travelling north together. A religious wedding had been out of the question and we had been given special permission to hold a civil ceremony in his home but all our plans had been thrown into chaos when, two weeks after our arrival, he went down with a bad bout of jaundice, only recovering in time to dash off to his job, leaving me behind with his mother and father.

Those early weeks in the country had been hugely exciting but the climate was physically debilitating and exposure to India's merciless deprivations emotionally draining. Everything was extreme. The light was painfully bright, colours vivid even strident, emotions volatile and vocal and smells pungent and pervasive. I was living in considerable comfort, visiting lavish homes and being taken to air-conditioned cinemas and restaurants but misery, death and disease were omnipresent and inescapable. Fi's parents lived in a reputedly quiet area but someone, somewhere, was always shouting and the endless cawing of crows formed a harsh backing group to these non-stop human voices. Even when everyone slept the otherwise welcome ceiling fans creaked and groaned through the night. I had longed for silence and – privacy. Life in the flat was very public. No-one ever closed a door and the family carried on their activities and conversations oblivious to servants who, seemingly always on duty, would suddenly and soundlessly appear but ignoring them made me uncomfortable. I did not have the language to greet them with a casual remark, and smiles and gestures felt inappropriate and unnecessarily ingratiating. I took to dressing in my bathroom, the only place where I could lock myself in, and on occasions even took a book and a cushion in there for a few quiet moments but it was never long before someone knocked on the door and asked if I was alright. Marooned among strangers, I had somehow survived all this without Fi until he had been able to snatch his recent, sketchy leave and return for me.

He had flown to Bombay on December the fourth and, at noon on the fifth, three months after our arrival in India, we had finally married. A table, covered with an embroidered cloth, had been placed in the centre of the large drawing room. The registrar, a small Maharashtrian in a white linen suit, spread out his register and papers with a combination of solemnity and fussiness. We sat down opposite him, two Parsi neighbours taking their seats on either side of us as witnesses and a group of aunts, uncles and cousins standing with Fi's parents and brother behind us. The brief formalities, conducted in English, were soon over and Fi's father whisked us and the registrar into his room. Bombay was relaxing its policy of total prohibition but alcohol was still scarce, costly and only available to permit holders and the four of us had a sneaky drink before re-joining the others for a more traditional rite.

"Aavo. Aavo. Come. Come." Fi's mother took my hand and led me across the room to a low, wide, wooden stool. "See. This is made from one piece of wood only with no joins, no divisions. It is our Parsi symbol of marriage. You must stand here. Firdaus! Aavo. Come here beside your wife."

We stood together on the stool. A cousin held out a round silver tray and my new mother-in-law dipped her finger into one of several small, fluted pots on this and anointed our foreheads with red marks. She then sprinkled us with rice from another pot before taking a pearl necklace and clasping it around my neck. She slid a matching bracelet on my arm and with a look of intense concentration clipped pearl studs on my ears. I had been told that she must, as was customary, give me a set of jewellery and had rashly opted for these tearful gems. After Fi's oldest aunt had put several bright glass bangles on my other arm, everyone surged forward to drape us with garlands and gifts until we began to look like small decorated Christmas trees. Beneath all this glitz, Fi was smart in a dark suit and tie and I wore a white silk dress with a pleated skirt that my mother had bought for me before I left home. My parents had never considered coming to my wedding for, even had it been a more acceptable event, India at that time seemed to them unimaginably distant and travel was extremely costly but, in spite of her rejection of Fi and her opposition to what I was doing, this dress, symbolic of just how torn my mother was, gave her a presence at a ceremony that she had dreaded. When Fi brought out a cameo brooch and pinned it on my collar, telling me that she had sent it to him with a note asking him to give it to me, the thought of the hidden pain and sadness behind everyone's determined cheerfulness rose like acid in my throat. All this ritual seemed suddenly like some play I was taking part in and it was only pride that held back my tears and kept me smiling.

Later, after an afternoon's rest, my father-in-law had hosted a splendid reception at the Taj Mahal hotel. Fi looked dashing and patriotic in a dark Nehru jacket and white trousers. I pleased everyone by wearing a sari, a gorgeous creation of cream raw silk with an interwoven border of purple and gold that is still stored, its beauty carefully packaged, in my present wardrobe, a matching three-quarter sleeved choli long since outgrown. I barely had time for any of the drinks or sumptuous cocktail snacks on offer at this party as I spent most of it shaking hands with guests: bidding farewell to the first arrivals shortly after taking a brief respite from welcoming late comers. Many of these people were strangers to me, government officials and businessmen important to my in-laws. The room was large and lit with glittering chandeliers and everyone was beautifully dressed, the women lavishly bejewelled, but, in a typically Indian juxtaposition of the sublime and the ridiculous, one of our servants was positioned behind our greeting line with a large shabby trunk, to collect and guard any wedding presents that we might be given.

The following evening, we stood on a station platform engulfed in a manic horde of thrusting bodies all moving urgently and unstoppably in different directions, screaming out instructions to friends and servants in a deafening, mind-numbing wave of sound. Fi and his father went off to supervise the fraught loading of our heavy baggage while we womenfolk waited next to the lighter luggage, surrounded by a crowd of porters in regulation red tunics and turbans, all vociferously touting for our custom. Once Fi returned, we chose one of the sturdier looking of these men, handed him a chit with our carriage number on it and followed him along the platform. The first time that you see your suitcases, piled on the cushioning turban of a frail, bow-legged man, disappearing in a sea of bobbing heads and gesticulating arms is a terrifying moment. You are sure that they are lost forever, but somehow, elbowing and jostling with all the energy of our fellow travellers, we managed to keep our man in view and to catch up with him as he stowed our things in our reserved coupe. A neat label on the door confirmed our new status: Mr and Mrs F.D. Khurody. We climbed aboard India's historic Frontier Mail and breathed an exhausted breath. Everyone crowded up to the window mouthing goodbyes, stepping hastily back, waving wildly, as the train hissed and shook itself before slowly sliding out of the noisy station and rattling off through the grimy outskirts of the city. We were on our way to Delhi, en route to a new life in a strange little town.

So! Here I was! It was no use sitting in the sun and dwelling on all this. My time in Bombay, the comparative luxury of my in-laws' home and urban pleasures were best forgotten for a while. That was yet another India and the only relevance of my time there was that it had, to a small degree, given me some insight into the influences that had made Fi what he was. We were starting out together from year zero with no other shared reality than our immediate sense of each other and our joint student life. Rural East Anglia where all my truest and deepest childhood experiences were rooted was as remote and foreign to him as this new country was to me. I was already half realising that from now on, wherever I lived, large tracts of my life would always be shut away inside me, unshared by the people I lived with.

I had to stop thinking. The immediate challenge was to do something, to convince myself that it was necessary and possible to do something positive and creative. I had no experience of domesticity but I had grown up with country women who were experts in housekeeping and home making and something seemed to have rubbed off on me. I aired our bedding in the sun to remove the worst of its chemical scent, remade our beds, put all our foodstuffs in order in the kitchen cupboards and set out our new rugs and cushions to good effect so that everything began to look a fraction less bleak. This did not take very long, however, and by the afternoon I resorted to a habitual source of comfort. I still had one or two of the paperbacks that I had borrowed from the guesthouse and taking a cane chair out into the courtyard, I settled down in the sunshine and was soon lost in one of these.

FOUR

I was still reading when I heard a vehicle pull up outside and was surprised to see Fi coming through the gate. He came across and bent to kiss me.

"Hello, Bookworm. Is this a wifely way to greet your husband? Come and see what I have brought back with me."

Outside, behind the jeep, stood a small truck with several of our crates in the back. The driver and two other factory workers were already unloading these and began to carry them through into the courtyard. Fi went back and, from under his seat, produced a large paper bag.

"Here's our dinner. No more sandwiches. We can have a real feast tonight. I've been to the piggery at the Dairy farm. I've got sausages and bacon. It's a bit difficult. We don't want to upset our landlord's religious sensibilities but hopefully he won't even recognise the smell when we cook them."

We opened all the boxes but only took out a minimum of crockery and cutlery, leaving everything else for me to unpack the next day. Fi caught me round the waist and kissed my cheek, holding up a second paper bag.

"I've got another surprise. I've been keeping it in my office until the right moment. Things look much better now and we actually have some glasses, so I think that this is the right moment."

He drew out a bottle of Johnny Walker whisky and two bottles of soda. "We'll continue the admirable custom of our erstwhile rulers, your countrymen, and have a chota peg before dinner."

Later, slightly fuzzy-headed and definitely cheered, we pumped up the paraffin stove. Its roars and hisses made this an alarming procedure that it would take me days to get used to but I braved it to produce somewhat charred sausages and fried potatoes while Fi grilled some bacon under our upturned electric ring. I set out cutlery, glasses and a bowl of fruit and we sat at our dining table and ate our first home-cooked food.

I must have prepared many meals in that terrible kitchen but though my recollection of that first one is so vivid that I can almost smell the sausages, I have no memory of what most of those others were like. Given the primitive appliances that I had, the limited ingredients available and the fact that I had never cooked anything other than basics like baked beans and eggs before, it must have been a boot camp cookery course and this was only one of the things that I had to learn.

Dealing with dates, commitments and appointments was an immediate and painful experience in an Eastern re-education of a Western sensibility. Time is subjective but for over twenty years I had been drilled in a military relationship with it. Speed and punctuality were my watchwords. Suddenly, like a small, caged animal frantically pedalling on a treadmill, I found that they got me nowhere. The Hindi word for 'now' is 'ubhi' but it proved to be a very open-ended term. 'Kul', the word for 'tomorrow', was equally slippery and unreliable. We had rented Dilkhusha for a month but with our factory bungalow in the relaxed hands of builders who used these terms in this typically casual way, we were actually there for nearly six months and it wasn't an easy time.

Even by local standards we had few facilities. I had always taken water for granted and now every drop we used involved enormous effort. Just making it fit for drinking was a complicated business. First we poured it into the top tier of a double ceramic container from which it slowly passed through a filter into the lower section. Then, after boiling it in a large pan on the paraffin stove and cooling it, we put it into cheap but beautiful earthen pots that kept it cool by a process of evaporation. The water we needed for general kitchen use was stored in two large drums in one corner of the room and there was a third drum in one of the outbuildings that stood in for a bathroom. To provide us with hot water, a local contractor made us an ingenious, circular contraption resembling an outsize tea urn. Every evening Fi would laboriously fill this from the hand pump and then light a fire in the central flue that ran through it. When the water was ready he carried it over to the outhouse in buckets. A simple, oriental, way to bath would have been to stand and pour water over ourselves from these buckets but habit is a compulsive thing and I was used to a tub, so we searched the bazaar and, among a heap of rickety, used items on sale at a roadside stall, found a somewhat rusty hip-bath. Bathing in this meant sitting on its raised end, my feet in the water-filled lower end, my knees high up under my chin, rinsing my body by using a large plastic jug to scoop hot water – from a bucket! For one very brief period, just before we finally left, we did actually have running water.

The monsoon arrived and, with rain pouring off the sloping roof and the guttering above the windows, we would snatch soap and flannels and rush out into the courtyard where, minus all respectability, we would scrub ourselves cool and clean.

Our other toilet needs were met by two wooden commodes in a second outhouse. These were fitted with removable basins that were emptied twice a day by a sweeper who carried the contents away to a pit in the field beyond the house. This pit seemed to serve the whole neighbourhood and some residents cut out the middleman and dealt directly with it. Looking out of the bedroom window into the dusty haze of early morning, I would always see several figures squatting around it with their metal water pots, apparently oblivious to onlookers and unselfconsciously engaging publicly in a function that I had been taught to see as something necessarily private. I had, though, grown up with the outdoor thunder boxes of rural Suffolk and, if I was obstinate over a bathtub, I was not daunted by our commodes. What I could not easily deal with was the daily sight of our sweeper coming across the field towards us to perform his unpleasant task. He was elderly and bent, with a slight limp and a squint in one eye. He wore a tattered dhoti, grubby shirt and a bright orange turban and carried a besom (a jharoo in Hindi) and a large bucket. Over time in India I hardened. I learned to close my eyes to many things. It was essential for survival. But this image physically pinched my heart and made my throat ache. He might have been a happy man with a wonderful family – the Indian capacity for happiness or, at least, an unresentful acceptance of misery, is astonishing – but I lacked the language and thus the skills to come close to people and nothing in my experience had prepared me for such an abstract icon of human dereliction and abject poverty. It made our lack of modern amenities seem trivial.

Fi was given the fulltime use of the jeep for as long as we remained in town and we did our shopping in the evenings when he came home from work. We followed a fixed route. We had discovered the spice market at the very top of the bazaar and always went there first to wander among the open sacks and baskets on display along the roadside. The shopkeepers sat cross-legged on roofed platforms above their wares, above the hubbub below them, their calm lamp-lit faces unmoved by the shrill bargaining of women in bright saris busily tapping and probing everything with their fingers. The distinctive smell of an Indian evening, a combination of dust, smoke, highly scented flowers, perfumes, the reek of Petromax lamps and the acrid aroma of chillies, stung our throats but the place had a special magic that always tempted us into lingering over our purchases of rice, dhal and herbs before setting off down the hill for "The Bombay General Store" to which we remained loyal. The ever cheerful owner was full of gossip and an unending interest in our affairs and always had an answer for everything. A remarkable number of the items we asked for seemed to cost exactly ten rupees. This, he informed us with wide-eyed solemnity, was "damn cheap". Fi never questioned the cost of something I wanted to buy without being told that it was damn cheap and quoted the price of an item in any shop, we would look at each other and mouth "DC". All the talk and laughter made going through our list a slow business but, with our groceries eventually bagged and paid for, we would go back to the bottom of the street for fruit and vegetables at the stalls there and before re-crossing the railway bridge, make a final stop at the Sikh's kiosk. This was not so much because we needed anything that he sold but because I had taken a liking to this impressive, dignified character.

By now we had completed all the home improvements we felt necessary for a temporary stay and were feeling more settled. I had rows of books on my bamboo bookshelf. Our record player, with a stack of records beside it, stood on an empty upended crate that I had disguised with a handloom cloth. Two smaller crates set on their sides, one on top of the other, formed a two-tier, box style storage unit for pots and pans in the kitchen and a fourth, placed in our "bathroom", with a large enamel bowl on it, served as a washbasin. We put this just inside the door so that any water we used could be thrown out directly onto the packed earth floor of the courtyard. What I had first taken to be a shower tray was in fact a dishwashing area but since it was too difficult to squat there and wash up, we made a similar arrangement in the kitchen with a larger bowl on yet another crate that made a more comfortable, if not totally adequate, sink.

All these problems dealt with reasonably satisfactorily, with books and music to ease any loneliness during my long, solitary days, we both felt that we had done the best we could for the time being. Like our shopping expeditions with their set pattern, our days fell into a routine. It is astonishing how quickly such regularity can make even the most bizarre situation seem normal. This began to seem less like a wild adventure and more like a life.

The factory was now fully up and running and going through all the teething problems that such new ventures throw up. Here, they were multiplied by the fact that this start-up was taking place in a remote area and involved a manufacturing process manned by an untried, inexperienced local work force. We never knew when Fi would have any free time but with the jeep at our disposal, we did use any time he had to explore the surrounding area and we began to get to know people and find people wanting to get to know us.

FIVE

I had not met all Fi's colleagues until a few days after our return from the Dairy Farm although, as we had stepped off the train onto the dusty platform on the day we arrived, a small, bouncy man had rushed up and clasped my hand.

"Joan. It is Joan? I'm your welcoming committee. Ozzie Castelino. Project Engineer. The man getting the factory up and running." He turned to Fi and slapped him on the shoulder. "Has this fellow told you much about us? He didn't tell us much about you. Keeping you as a pleasant surprise I see. Celine, my wife, is very keen to meet you but we've decided to let you settle in before we have a get-together. Fi, there's trouble at the plant right now. I can't leave my chaps too long. Have to get back. I'll take the jeep. The car and driver are yours for the rest of the day. They are waiting outside. We'll see you soon Joan. Don't worry. Everyone is anxious to meet you and we'll be in touch."

"Ozzie's a Catholic from Goa," Fi said, watching him strut off. "I don't know about his faith in God but he certainly believes in himself. You'll like Celine though. She's a quiet, sensible person. Also a Catholic of course."

"Catholic? But they are Indians surely."

"Goa belongs to the Portuguese and they converted or perhaps in the early days even married some of the locals.

That's why there are Indians with names like Castelino. Well, it seems we are on our own. They all want to leave us to ourselves for a while and we'll be going….." He broke off and took my arm. "Well we'll get to see them in time. After all we are on our honeymoon."

"Some honeymoon!" I snorted.

"Well, I admit that neither the Frontier Mail nor this place seems very romantic but we have had some honeymoonish moments, haven't we?"

I laughed. "Yes we have but I do want to meet all these people. I'm going to have to live with them for a long time after all."

When we did finally meet everyone, it was not at Dilkhusha but in their homes. Dr Saraswat, the Hindu manager, was living with his wife, Vidhya, and their two children in a substantial bungalow about a mile away from us. The Castelinos occupied the upper floor of a pleasant house nearby that was currently serving as an interim company headquarters with one room kept free for visitors. It was this room that Fi had occupied until now. Since their landlord lived on the ground floor, the house was well maintained and orderly. Both families had been in the town for over a year, from the start of the building work on the factory site. Clearly they had needed to be comfortable and because they had been able to take out longer leases on their houses than was necessary for us, had found reasonable places. Still, I suspected that they felt some discomfort at facing our less than adequate accommodation with its many deficiencies only too apparent and impossible to ignore. The fact that I was English probably didn't help matters. It made for an unusual situation. They were working for an English company whose senior managers were Englishmen. Though Dr Saraswat with his PhD was the local manager, the overall authority would for some time rest with a General Manager, working from Delhi or from Bombay headquarters. The unacknowledged fact, reinforced by the hard realities of remuneration, was that even high grade Indian employees were second rank, though in this small town environment their association with a foreign company gave them considerable standing and opened doors for them among the local elite. I never, in all my years in India, encountered any overt anti-English feeling, certainly not at a personal level, but the relationship between the two nationalities had its history and ambivalences and could probably never be entirely straightforward and without its sharp edges, though it is true that many of these had largely been rubbed smooth by the long abrasion of that shared history.

As a couple, Fi and I had crossed a boundary and, in that place and time, were certainly something of an anomaly. This was probably less difficult for our new friends because Fi was also in a way an outsider. The Parsis, Indians by virtue of a centuries-long residence and acquired habits, were in fact Persian immigrants, followers of the onetime state religion of ancient Persia with its tombs and monuments still standing in modern Iran, who around the seventh or eighth century had fled the Islamisation of their country by its Arab conquerors. They were a small and successful minority group holding on to a distinct and separate identity and even though they had adopted an Indian language – Gujarati – they had put their own idiosyncratic stamp on it. So, if our Hindu and Moslem friends took time to feel totally at ease with us, they did not have to deal with the problem of our having broken any of their own specific social or religious taboos.

Dr Saraswat threw a welcome party for me, inviting several local officials and businessmen and their wives and treating us all to a delicious vegetarian meal. At first everyone was a little stiff and formal but that changed once we sat down to eat. Indians love to feed people but are always anxious about a stranger's reactions to their food. Even those who have lived there for years and eaten endless curries are still continually asked, "How do you like our food? Is our food too hot for you?" That evening I was urged to try a particular delicacy, small pastry balls that looked to me like puffed up, miniature Yorkshire puddings.

"Just make a hole in them and put this inside." I was handed a jug of some pungent liquid.

"It's pepper sauce. It's very good. Very tasty."

Everyone turned to watch me as I pierced my first pastry and poured in the sauce. I swallowed it and gasped for breath. I was sweating and my face was bright red.

"Fire Brigade! Fire Brigade for Mrs Khurody," everyone shouted excitedly.

My hostess handed me a bowl of vermicelli cooked in milk and sugar and told me to eat a few mouthfuls. This instantly soothed my raw throat. I breathed normally again and they all smiled delightedly. From that moment they relaxed, chatting easily with me and treating me with a sort of tender indulgence. I had been polite and ready to try their food but it was a little too much for me. It was just as they had expected.

We create stereotypes to reduce complexity to simplicity and to construct a working model of the world that enables us to get by in it without overtaxing ourselves. It's like flipping through an illustrated book rather than getting to grips with a densely written text. Nowadays, of course, we no longer have to make much effort to read the world anyway. It is all done for us by television. If we have additional queries we can go online. Even the place that I am recalling, which seemed to me at the time to be so far away that I felt as if I had travelled to Timbuctoo, has its own website. Students probably spend gap years there. Once, our window onto the world was much narrower and most people rarely travelled abroad. Until I set sail from Liverpool, I had never been out of England. Today, when Africa, China, India and many other countries, glide past our sitting room chairs in High Definition, like the scenery viewed from a coach window, when people from the remotest villages appear to actually speak to us face to face, it is impossible to describe how unreal such places were to girls from my working class background. We were highly educated, first generation college students with good A levels in geography but our certificated knowledge consisted of a collection of dry facts rather than any understanding of what actual lives in the countries that we studied were like. I had a picture of an Indian woman, sari-clad, with a smooth serene face, almond eyes and a finely chiselled nose, her hair sleekly pulled back into a luxuriant bun and her hands demurely folded. Now I faced the real thing.

Vidhya Saraswat had a square face, a broad somewhat upturned nose and a wide, flexible mouth that could stretch into a wicked grin or droop discontentedly, as her changing moods drove her. Her hair was cut into a shoulder length bob that could, on occasions like our first party, be drawn back as sleekly as I expected but it usually flew about with all the somewhat wild energy she herself was capable of. The white saris she wore did give her the air of a traditional Hindu wife but she often took down the pallu from her shoulders and tied it about her waist to give her more freedom of movement and it was difficult to see her being demure or obedient. I rather felt that her husband, who could be very aware of his status and stand on his dignity with workers or lesser men, was somewhat careful around her. Celine Castelino, on the other hand, who generally wore western dresses and court shoes or heeled sandals, had exactly the smooth, serene face I had expected. Her hair was drawn neatly back in a pleat or a bun, her manner was sweet and gentle and she constantly deferred to her rather bombastic little husband.

I needed to get along with everyone but with these two women in particular. We would soon be neighbours on a claustrophobic, out-of-the-way site and unusually dependant on each other. Since they both had a longer association with this town than I had and were in their own country, I would be the most vulnerable of the three of us and there would be inevitable tensions because we would be a very introverted group, living in enforced proximity, with our personal and working lives too interwoven for complete ease. So it felt good when Fi and I began to make friends in the town itself.

The morning after the party, I heard a knock on the gate and peering cautiously out of the bedroom window, saw a slight, balding Englishman in his forties standing outside. I rushed to let him in. He was a welcome sight and had welcome things to tell me. His name was Don Long and he was the padre of a small Anglican church with a tiny congregation of Indian Christians.

"The church is about a mile from here and we have a pleasant bungalow in the compound. 'We' means myself, my wife, Wyn, and our small son, David. We're the only English family in the town so Wyn was really delighted to hear about your arrival. It's a bit short notice but she can't wait to meet you. I've been sent to invite you and your husband to supper tomorrow evening."

His unaccented voice with no vestige of trills or upward inflections had a strange effect on me. Tongues and lips fall effortlessly into the shapes and positions of a native language and minds seem to function in the same way. There is a rush of ease and spontaneity when meeting a countryman after a time among strangers. I longed to burst into endless questions, to launch into my life history without restraint. I was bursting with unspoken things that needed to be spoken but recalling Eva's outburst when we met, I forced myself to be sensible.

When he left, I had not only accepted his invitation to supper the next evening but had promised that we would also go to church for the next service. I had no qualms about committing Fi to this. He was a Zoroastrian by birth and custom but was a complete agnostic. I came from a line of militant Methodists but although my mother had already rebelled against their straitlaced ways and brought me up without religion, I had a purely aesthetic love of Anglican rituals acquired during my years in a primary church school and I had an internal repertory of both Anglican and Methodist hymns that were a joy. Fi, who had taken voice training lessons in England and loved to sing, always managed to find time for music. It was the thought of an outlet for this shared pleasure and a sense of national solidarity that made me agree to our joining Don and his congregation for Sunday worship.

The following day, as I was looking through my wardrobe and planning what to wear that evening, there was another knock at the gate. This time when I went to my spy station, I saw two Indian women in cotton saris and woollen jackets standing at the gate, talking quietly to each other. Apparently the institution at the bend of the road was a Muslim college for girls and they were both teachers there, though they themselves were Catholics and came from Kerala. They had surprisingly English names. One was Miss Thomas and the other Miss Joseph. I invited them in but they told me that they were on their way back to classes and, having heard that there was an English lady living here, had only stopped by to introduce themselves and to invite me for tea with them. I said that I would love to come for tea and they promised to fetch me at about three o'clock the next afternoon.

That evening, as we drove into the Long's compound and followed the drive under the domed porch that extended beyond their door, I was reminded of the Dairy Farm bungalow. This was not a long, elegant building. It was square and solid but it had the same aura. A bougainvillea was trained up one wall and there was an array of pot plants on the steps. The Longs came out to meet us, their small blonde son clinging to his mother's skirt. She disengaged him and came down the steps to take my hand.

"Joan. Hello. How lovely to meet you. It's so good to see someone from home."

Once again I was overwhelmed by a weak and watery feeling. It seemed to be voices that were affecting me. Wyn's was low, with a hint of Northern England about it but no frills. As she stood close to me, she even smelled familiar. I caught a combination of Ponds Cold cream and Eau de Cologne.

"I've let David stay up to see you but he's going straight to bed now. When he heard about you, he asked if you could read him a bedtime story. I do rather annoy our cook because I like to do something towards feeding our guests and I thought you might read to David while I pop into the kitchen. Would you?"

Sitting beside the low bed reading "Peter Rabbit" as Fi and Don chatted over a drink and Wyn went off to check on our meal, it felt as if I had undergone one of those miraculous transportations of science fiction. I could have been in England. For supper, we had tomato soup, roast chicken and blancmange. It was like Sunday lunch at home.

India isn't that easily defeated. Over coffee, Don began to tell us stories, the kind of stories that are part of every ex-pat's conversational repertoire. Today, most of them would probably be untellable, branded racist. I know that people are complicated and contradictory but I do wonder if it is possible to truly love your Indian congregation, live with them far from your home, work tirelessly to deal with their physical as well as their spiritual needs and still be a racist. Is it possible to marry someone of another race and commit to that someone's country and be a racist? It's all very well to sit comfortably in a liberal Western world among liberal Western friends and set rules for the rest of humanity but there are nuances here. Most of these stories were an equal mixture of gentle criticism and genuine affection. Even the less defensible of them served as safety valves for the tensions and grievances that are unavoidable when different groups really do live together and not merely in a carefully positioned proximity. It was a kind of mild bloodletting that staved off anything more harmful.

As he quoted sections of an application letter that he was supposed to have received, Don knew that this was standard stuff. Everyone claimed to have received such a letter, the legendary stock in trade of professional letter writers: "Dear Sir, I live two miles from you as the cock crows….. If you give me this post, I will leave no stone unturned to serve you….. I have three children by your kindness…… I will do all your works both honourable and dishonourable."

His face creased with laughter at thinking of such a promise being made to a man of the cloth.

"But what is a man of the cloth to them? And speaking of the cloth, I've actually seen our dhobi wearing my cassock in the bazaar."

"Come on." Fi protested. "You are making that up."

"No. It's a useful multi-purpose garment. He collects it with all the laundry on a Monday, wears it, washes it and returns it in time for the Sunday services. We both get good use out of it."

We did not totally believe this story but Don very much enjoyed telling it and Wyn was smiling at him, encouraging him to prolong this special pleasure.

"Tell them the story about our watchman. You know. What happened when we came back from Delhi recently."

Don turned to us. "Don't think that we gad off to Delhi often. We only go about twice a year but we did make one of those trips last month and we came home quite late to find the chowkidar asleep in the front porch. Hearing the car, he leapt up and rushed to open the door. Do you know what he said? 'Sorry Sahib. I was round the back.' What a gift for improvisation. I just love that imaginative streak in these men."

There were more stories but it was getting late and we had to leave. We went home warm and contented, very pleased to have found such agreeable friends.

The next afternoon, Miss Thomas came to fetch me for tea. Her friend had stayed behind to prepare things. We walked across the field and came to a small back gate in the college wall. Both the women had quarters just inside this, on the outskirts of the compound. I never did know if this was a form of religious segregation but I was shocked by the drab discomfort in which they lived. It was Dilkhusha in miniature and both of them had made similar efforts to cheer things up. We visited both sets of rooms but ate in Miss Joseph's. She had put a beautiful cutwork cloth on her cheap table and set a pottery vase of flowers in the centre of an array of doily covered plates heaped with various kinds of thin sandwiches, pastries and highly coloured buns. We sat on somewhat rickety cane chairs made comfortable with soft, gaily embroidered seat cushions. There were rag rugs on the uneven stone floor and family photographs and religious pictures on all the walls.

Miss Thomas was the younger of the two and taught mathematics. She was a very solid woman with a slightly overbearing manner and a deep, emphatic voice. She was probably about thirty and good-looking in a hearty, healthy way with tightly coiled, jet black curls round a plump, rosy face. Miss Joseph was smaller, older and quieter. She had looser curls already grey and turning white. As we met more frequently and I saw her overshadowed by her ebullient, self-confident companion, she seemed to personify the exhaustion of a life spent working far from home, living in grim conditions and earning very little measureable reward, a warning of what even Miss Thomas might come to. It was a crass, hasty observation. I soon realised that, although her life was hard and often lonely and that it became even lonelier when, shortly after they first visited me, Miss Thomas left for a post in Delhi, Miss Joseph had many inner resources. If she was an object lesson for Miss Thomas, she was also one for me. She taught English literature and I had a degree in English and Philosophy and we were soon spending happy hours together, reading, discussing and dissecting the books that we both enjoyed. These rather highbrow sessions drew us closer until we also began sharing far more personal confidences, a sharing that comforted and sustained us both.

Fi was pleased and, more importantly, relieved to see me finding companionship. He could now go off to the factory with less anxiety and feel freer to concentrate on his job. He was lucky at such an early stage in his working life to be involved in an experimental and ground-breaking project. A product, baby food, long imported, was being developed here, adapting and using local materials for the first time and employing local labour. Indian expertise, including his own, was playing a large part in this. He was understandably eager to get on with things and not having to leave me so alone made this a good deal easier for him.

Christmas came upon us so soon after our arrival that it took me by surprise and in these surroundings I couldn't quite believe in it. We had a muted day. The factory was only briefly closed and after a church service, a simple lunch with the Longs and a drive out to the farm with gifts for Taj Massi and the other servants who insisted on giving us tea and sweets, we ended the day alone, listening to music in our far from festive living room. Fi very carefully chose records that were unlikely to encourage a slightly tearful tendency in me.

I was already meeting the other wives quite often. Vidhya was living among Hindu families with whom she had much in common but Celine, a Christian accustomed to the ways of Portuguese Goa was, surprisingly, almost as far from home as I was and we spent a lot of time together, with Vidhya occasionally joining us for morning coffee. Fi and I were, though, quickly building on the core of our outside social circle to offset any more incestuous relationship with the company staff. By the middle of our second month we were going to church on Sunday mornings and getting to know the regular congregation. Most weeks we had Sunday lunch with the Longs, who quite understood the impossibility of our asking them back for a serious meal. Tea parties were less of a problem and there was soon a regular back and forth between the college rooms and Dilkhusha. With the help of a special griddle used for making chapattis and a recipe book that my mother-in-law sent me, I even began to make scones and Welsh cakes on my paraffin stove. With the feeling of solidity and normality that having friends gave us, we next looked to see what entertainments the town provided.

SIX

In mid-January, shortly after Miss Thomas had dropped the sudden bombshell of her transfer and gone off to Delhi, Miss Joseph arrived one day looking uncharacteristically animated. She had considerable depth but her surface was usually placid and unruffled and it was a surprise to hear her excitable tones.

"Guess what, my dear." She sounded quite breathless as if she had rushed over from her rooms. "I'm told that someone has opened a coffee shop in the bazaar and that it has the very latest espresso machines. When Fi is next free, I want to treat you both to a coffee there."

It says something about the amenities on offer that such a staid and serious lady should be so thrilled at the thought of our having this coffee together and she was still in an unusually heightened state on the day that we went off to have it. The new place was a few yards beyond our general store and seemed to have created quite a stir. Its small space was dominated by a boarded semi-circular counter with the touted espresso machines and some pastries wilting under domed glass covers on it. There was only room for half a dozen bright plastic tables and chairs and we had to wait to sit at one of these. The owner wrote our order on a white pad with a flourish and went to get the coffee and cakes that we wanted. At this point there was a sudden uproar as two large rats shot across the floor, ran behind the counter and began to fight ferociously. A series of shrieks and thumps as they continually banged against its sides, rose above the hiss of the machines and the loud conversation at the other tables. Fi gave me a look as I tried to stay serious and we valiantly continued small talk with our poor friend and even more valiantly ate the pastries that came with our coffee. But she was nothing if not a realist. As she paid the bill and we rose to leave, she said. "There is nothing to beat good manners. Thank you, my dears, for being so considerate. I'm truly sorry that it has all been such a disappointment." I bent over and kissed her cheek. "It's been an experience and you've given me a story to tell for years to come."

Undeterred by this farcical outing, I decided that I would like to go to the cinema. All over town, garish posters advertising Hindi films depicted narrow-waisted women with astonishing bosoms. They had the hour glass figures of corseted Victorians displayed in all the bare- midriff freedom of a sari. Most of them seemed to be peering coyly round trees at men almost as beautiful as themselves. I wanted to see if these stars could possibly be like this in the flesh or at least in celluloid action.

"In the flesh is about right." Fi shook his head at me. "They all look very 'healthy' as my mother would say. You do realise that all these stories are highly improbable, the acting will be over the top and there will be endless dancing and some very shrill music all the way through. Anyway you won't understand a word of it all."

I was making a real effort to learn the language with the help of a Hindustani grammar and a phrase book and I got a little cross.

"Don't be so negative. Even if I can't understand much I'll get a feel for the language. It could help me to follow dialogue and conversation"

In the end we went off to the shabby cinema on the spur of the moment one evening, only to find that the film then showing was not in fact a gaudy melodrama but a version of the Ramayana, a Hindu epic poem telling stories of battles between gods and demons. We arrived just as it was about to start and ran up the stairs to the circle, where we found that we formed the entire audience. The seats were all strange little doubles, like small, poorly upholstered sofas. This puzzled me. It seemed highly unlikely that the kind of thing that went on in the back rows of English cinemas would be possible in this strict society. We both sat primly upright in our shared seat. The credits rolled, superimposed on an image of Hanuman the monkey god sitting on his fabled tail or what looked to me rather more like a large coil of rope. At that moment, a sudden movement on the edge of my vision made me turn from the screen. I shrieked and clutched Fi's arm. A rat had run down the far wall and landed on the floor with an unpleasant thud.

"It's alright. It won't come near us." Fi patted my hand. "They mostly avoid people."

"What about all those stories of pavement sleepers being bitten?"

I pushed him away and made him move onto a separate seat so that I could tuck my feet up under me, unconvinced that we were safe. As I had insisted on coming I made an effort to concentrate on the film but when the horrible creature ran jauntily along the seats two rows in front of us, jumping from one to the other, I gave up.

"That's it. Let's go." I headed for the exit, looking over my shoulder as I went.

The usher had just settled down in the back row to enjoy the film himself and ran into the doorway in front of us, blocking our way and waving his arms excitedly. "No. No, Memsahib. Film is just starting. Very good film."

"Memsahib is not well." Fi gently moved him aside and we escaped into the grimy car park and headed home.

Coffee shops and cinemas were out. We tried to entertain ourselves at home. It was lucky that we had our records. Fi had a largely classical collection and we could happily spend an evening with Beethoven and Mozart echoing incongruously around our whitewashed walls. My own collection was a more ragtag affair and I sometimes played a pathetic song by Lonnie Donegan called "I'm Nobody's Child" until, sickened by my sentimental wallowing in manufactured misery, I turned to my favourite Flamenco records. Their blend of passion, stirring rhythm and haunting pathos matched my own jumbled feelings and chimed far more genuinely with my mood. Farid Khan, who could hear these high pitched sounds even through Dilkhusha's thick walls, was not impressed.

"What is this terrible music you play, Mrs Khurody? It is like listening to seven goats in a field having their throats cut."

I spent hours studying and reading. My academic leanings were a blessing. I had a new language to learn and the history of my new country to discover. I also had most of my special loves with me, books that could be read and reread, but I still sometimes felt a need for something new and there was no bookshop in the town. The only place to go was the station bookstall. Passing through Bombay Central Station, a huge closed terminus, I had choked on a potent odour of mingled humanity, coal smoke and urine and though on our small open platform it was less pervasive, this smell still hung in the air and was far from the agreeable aroma of new paper and print that I associated with book buying. The stall itself backed against the station wall and was six feet long with a canopied counter about three feet wide, displaying a disproportionate number of Agatha Christie and Erle Stanley Gardner paperbacks and, inexplicably, many of Zane Grey's cowboy tales and the florid romances of Marie Corelli. It was not a particularly impressive structure but was, nevertheless, part of an historic institution. A.H.Wheeler, an Indian company shaped by the unlikely combined input of a French author and an Indian businessman and named after a successful bookshop in London, had set up its first bookstall on Allahabad station in 1877. At first most of the books it stocked were English publications and its customers also English but slowly books in various Indian languages were introduced, opening an outlet for Indian writers and a supply of reading matter for local populations. Licenced by the British Raj, the company held a monopoly on book sales at stations for years, a monopoly recently rescinded. Today, there are still arguments raging around it, questions over the kind of books it sells and criticism of its increasing tendency to fill its stalls with flashy magazines. Whatever the rights or wrongs of its modern status and activities, for over a century, it was the only source of reading matter in the many small towns where it operated and it was certainly a life saver for me.

In spite of my bookish inclinations, I was also very much an outdoor girl. All my relatives were country people and I had spent my summers on my grandfather's Suffolk farm. My father was an avid reader who had fostered my love of books but he was also an out and out countryman and had always belonged to a shooting syndicate. Fi too had uncles and relatives who either lived outside Bombay or had small country properties and outings to these places had been very much a part of his boyhood. He had been a boarder at one of India's most prestigious schools, the Doon School in Dehradun, whose first headmasters came from Eton and Harrow and brought with them not only elements of public school training but also a very English love of the sporting life. At the foot of the Himalayas and surrounded by forests, the school offered great opportunities for field, fishing and shooting trips and Fi had been on many of these during half term holidays. Until now, we had only shared academic and largely urban pursuits but one of the good things about our restricted cultural opportunities was this discovery of a shared enjoyment of rural life.

Our town was situated in Uttar Pradesh and a swathe of the Indo-Gangetic plain with its jheels or small lakes and canal system became our leisure park. It was a seemingly untouched, empty place but it was actually densely populated and highly agricultural and the amazing thing was that however far from habitation we sometimes thought ourselves, whenever we stopped to eat or, more embarrassingly, to squat in a sugar cane field, someone would almost always suddenly appear as if out of the ground and give us quite a fright. Often as we spread the car rug and opened our lunch packets, a small gathering of villagers would quickly form around us. We were a rare source of entertainment and they sat around commenting on us and speculating openly about who or what we could possibly be. Our unmatched and odd appearance was clear evidence that we could not possibly understand what they were saying.

During the winter months from December to late February, we covered huge tracts of the flat countryside and I must admit to an occasional nervous moment as we drove along bumpy tracks with little idea of where we were or where we were going but however lost we were and however bad these tracks became, Fi had a dogged determination to see things through and could become quite impatient if I showed any faintheartedness. He was only twenty five, with all a young man's sense of adventure – and a girl to impress – but given that I was here at all, I had to suppress a pang that he could ever doubt my courage. I did have to admit that we always found our way home eventually even if it was in darkness with the stars our only guide. Only once were we caught out.

We were following a sandy lane that had clearly been used mainly, if not solely, by bullock carts with heavy loads and over years the wheel ruts had deepened on each side of a central ridge. The jeep began to struggle. Fi refused to turn back, insisting that we would find our way onto a better road. Suddenly we stopped. The jeep was suspended on the ridge, its wheels turning helplessly like the waving legs of a stranded insect. This time I was genuinely upset and scared. It was dark and there seemed to be nothing but fields for miles all around. Even in daylight the space we drove through looked boundless but, with no visible markers, it expanded into the darkness endlessly. No one popped up to see us now. It felt very lonely and even dangerous. I told myself that of course there were no lions and tigers but there were jackals in the area. I had heard their eerie calls.

"What shall we do?" My voice was shaky.

"Well," Fi sounded calm, "if bullock carts have worn the track down, it means that it leads to a village. We'll go and find someone to help us. They'll have lights and spades. They'll be able to dig us out."

We stumbled along. Unlikely as it seems now, I still always wore dresses or skirts and my legs, even in heavy stockings, felt very exposed. My imagination played with images of horrors like scorpions and snakes. Luckily we soon saw the vague outline of darkened houses and Fi stopped and shouted out, anxious to warn people of our approach.

"Arre Bhai! Hello brother! Koi Hai? Is there anyone there?"

A faint, shaky voice called back from the nearest house and Fi gave a snort of laughter.

"He's telling us to take everything but to spare his life. He thinks we're bandits."

"Bandits!" I hissed. "No-one mentioned bandits."

Everyone had been keen to impress on me the hazards of this place but had failed to tell me about any such extreme danger. Here was I worrying about wild animals and creeping things and there might be vicious thieves about. I found it difficult to take this possibility completely seriously but Fi was not entirely reassuring.

"Well, armed gangs certainly do operate in remote parts of all these northern states. When I was a boy, we used to drive up to Dehra Dun from Bombay through one particular gorge, a noted haunt of dacoits as we called them, where we always had to wait to join with other cars and pass through in convoy in case of attacks. But, don't worry. It's highly unlikely that we'll ever face such problems. This is simply a nervous villager's overheated response to the unexpected arrival of strangers in what to him is the middle of the night."

He began walking up to the house making soothing conversation and a man wrapped in a thin blanket finally came out. I don't know how this was cleared up, as most of the exchange was beyond my elementary vocabulary but eventually, I was left with a group of sleepy women who tut-tutted over me, stroked my arms and gave me water while Fi went off with a group of men carrying mattocks, spades and lanterns. They returned about an hour later, most of them either in or hanging onto, the jeep. Fi offered them whatever money he had with him but clearly this was very little since we had no need of money on such jaunts. In any case they refused with great dignity and said that it was rare for Burra log or Big people to notice them and all they asked was that we should remember them and come again to see them.

Over the next seven years our picnics and expeditions would play a large part in our lives. Recalling that wide, sunlit landscape with its huge open skies and the pleasant winter days when we roamed over it, I feel again just how at home I became there. This was a kind of 'Garden of Eden' experience of the country. That is an exaggerated image but it does evoke not only this seemingly unspoilt, rural backdrop but my own ignorance and innocence. I am probably guilty of distortion here. Memory, as I have said, is a strange thing. My time there is sometimes bathed in this happy afterglow but, in fact, there were long, lonely hours to get through and a great deal of frustration. Some days, seeing Fi go off to the factory to spend his time with equally qualified men, all of them sharing in the same task and all jointly committed to it, I felt a severe pang at the thought of my own hopes and plans indefinitely on hold, with only the prospect of a tea party or a supper to console me. It was impossible not to envy his chance to use his abilities and qualifications. I had so recently been part of a lively academic community, sharing living quarters with students of my age and there were so many things that I sorely missed: mental stimulation; discussions with friends who shared interests and a history with me; familiar radio programmes; libraries; theatres; plays, ballet and musicals; cinemas without rats. I always told myself firmly that I had chosen this course and especially in those early months, it was not without its excitements and rewards. There was a constant stream of novel impressions to process even if there were also long stretches of sheer boredom to endure.

It was fortunate that I had come to this town at a good time. All our hardships were less trying because of the winter weather. It was a little chilly when I took my bath in our outhouse but that was one of the only drawbacks of the season. Now there was a monsoon and a summer to deal with.

SEVEN

There was no sudden change of season but winter died away and the days warmed up gradually. Although in March the temperature reached the eighties at the height of the day, the air was dry and it was not unbearable. There was a time from the end of February until late April when both the weather and our life went through a slow, relatively uneventful period.

I hadn't seen Eva since before Christmas. Then, one Sunday afternoon as Fi was pumping water and I was standing at the gate waiting to carry my share inside, the whole family came bumping across the rough ground towards us in their ancient, open-topped Baby Austin, Mike square and expressionless in the driving seat, Eva beside him, curls and arms waving and their three girls sitting high in the rear seat. They came to a halt against the wall.

"The brakes aren't all they might be," said Mike calmly and we suddenly understood the reason for a gouged patch on the wall of their own otherwise immaculate bungalow that had always puzzled us. It was their regular stopping point.

The girls, who ranged in age from eight to thirteen, jumped from the car and ran inside to explore our poor home with shrill cries.

"Mrs Khurody, don't say that this is really your bath. Mrs Khurody, do you cook here yourself? Don't you have a servant?"

Their father quieted them and apologised. "They are young barbarians. Why I pay what I do to school them I can't think. But you should have some help, Joan. We could find someone for you. There are relatives of our workers living in town who would be glad of a job."

I had been putting off dealing with this issue. There were moral and practical factors involved that made it hard for me. I had been brought up to believe that it was wrong to ask other people to do jobs that you were capable of doing but disliked and the early hints of a budding feminism notwithstanding, the fact that most domestic servants were male somehow made doing so more unpalatable. In my in-laws' flat in Bombay, I had found myself continually falling over cooks, sweepers and bearers and the lack of privacy had been hard to get used to. Here in our cramped quarters it was impossible to accommodate anyone. The only place for a servant to sleep would be the third outhouse and apart from considerations of his comfort, there was the problem of its closeness to our toilet facilities. I was making do with the sweeper. Even my refined conscience balked at doing his job. I did some minimal cleaning and very simple cooking and felt that I was managing alright. Mike insisted that my western views were not quite in tune with the realities. Everyone felt uncomfortable if you did not behave according to your status, including the people that you considered put upon if they did things that you did not want to do. The blunt fact was that they needed work. Young men had no choice but to do domestic chores in order to live and if you could afford to pay their wages it was almost your duty to do so. I saw the force of this and agreed to take on the nephew of one of the farm workers. His name was Gopal and he lived in the town and could come in daily for three hours each morning to sweep the floors, wash dishes, pump water and run small errands into the bazaar for me. There was a bit of a tussle over what we should pay him. I wanted to be generous, especially since it was my choice to curtail the hours on offer, but again I was made to face up to hard facts. If I paid more than was usual, Gopal himself would face some degree of envy from his family and friends that would make things difficult for him and if he ever left us and worked elsewhere or we ever went away, he would find it hard to adjust to more stringent conditions. Local families might well be unable to afford what we could pay. The going rates had to be adhered to for everyone's sake. There were no easy solutions in this constant balancing act that pitted my instinctive reactions against the new world I was dealing with. The best I could do was pay the maximum possible that would not cause problems, treat people I employed with consideration and respect and give as much as I could in kind whenever an opportunity arose.

One very real benefit for me of having Gopal around all morning was that I got a chance to practice spoken Hindi, or more accurately, Hindustani. This hybrid of Hindi and Urdu is widely used in the North and has its origins in an influx of Persian and Arabic speakers around the thirteenth century and a consequent mingling of Persian, Arabic, Sanskrit and various local dialects. It was the language widely used by the British Raj and the phrasebook that I had on hand at all times was produced for British officials and military men. I was now able to give simple instructions and even begin to make some general conversation, though my tongue stumbled over certain sounds and there were glitches from time to time. I once asked Gopal to buy some cream. In my book I found the word for this – malai – and tried it out in various forms while he looked at me uncomprehendingly. I must have suddenly hit on the right pronunciation for his face lit up. "Ah, cream!" he said, his farm connections apparent. From then on, whenever Fi or I caught on to something being explained to us, we would say, "Ah, cream!"

Having domestic help made me feel that I needed to up my game and do something more ambitious as a housewife. I decided that I would try a roast chicken dinner and invited the Longs, still the only people I dared to expose to my cooking, for my first ever formal meal. So far we had largely eaten tinned foods, vegetables and pork products from the farm piggery. Fish was unavailable and, because we had always eaten it regularly at home and I had so recently sampled the wonderful seafood of Bombay, this was a real deprivation. Somehow tinned sardines, the only fish that we could get, were not quite the same. I had eaten beef (which was buffalo) and mutton (which was goat) at other homes and found it all tough and strongly flavoured even when curried. My feeling, rightly or wrongly, was that Indian animals were exploited to the full and then, their usefulness at an end, their muscles stringy and their flesh falling away, they were slaughtered and eaten. I had almost lost my appetite for meat and when on one of our excursions to the bazaar, Fi took me to a butcher's shop for the first time, I almost turned vegetarian on the spot. It was a tiny little place, its entrance covered by a reed screen that was black with flies. I remembered my grandfather singing a song called "Where do flies go in the wintertime?" This seemed to be the answer. Inside, a bearded man in a blood-stained dhoti sat in the centre of the floor, on one end of a long narrow board. At the other end of this, there was a fixed, upright blade which he held firm with the toes of one foot as he cut slices from a slab of meat. I hastily backed out and left Fi to explain that we were in the wrong place.

So I decided on a chicken. I asked Gopal to go into the bazaar and buy it for me. Still incredibly naïve, I expected him to bring back a prepared bird such as I had seen my mother deal with. This one was alive and squawking loudly in protest at being slung under his arm. I hid in the kitchen until further, louder squawks finally petered out and I was presented with a scrawny, badly plucked creature. I pulled at the remaining feathers on it without much effect, washed it and placed it gingerly in the pressure cooker that I had taken out of our crates. After what I estimated to be a reasonable time, it emerged pallid and unappetising, with its wings crossed on its breast, looking quite sacrificial. In desperation, I put it in the frying pan and turned it over and over until it was a pale brown shade but when I tried to put a fork into it, I found it so hard and rubbery that I gave up. We had dhal, rice and vegetable curry for dinner. This was everyday fare but Wyn and Don politely said that they enjoyed it and we all enjoyed each other's company. There was no one else with whom we could have been so easy in such circumstances.

Our landlord would often appear at the gate soon after Fi got home and sit with us to discuss life and literature and the settlement of the electricity bill, our share of which he computed in a way we never understood. As our stay was extended, he came up with an idea to give us running water and continually went over the details of this with Fi. His plan was to fix a small motor to the hand pump and run a pipe from this up to a tank on the roof from which water would flow through a second pipe down to the house. He bought a large petrol drum to serve as a tank and did actually get a workman to fix a pipe up to the roof but when we finally left, this was still trailing down the wall, open at both ends and the drum was lying on its side in the courtyard. He knew that we had thought about getting a car and said that he had one or two that only needed some slight repairs. We thought of the derelict wrecks outside and blenched. Once, shifting his bulk uncomfortably on our insubstantial cane chair, he told us he also had a three piece suite that, with new covers, would be just the thing for us. Taking a stool outside one day, I climbed up to inspect the marshy wasteland behind the courtyard that he called his garden. There stood the three piece suite, in a mini forest of reedy grasses, its springs bursting through its faded upholstery and its stuffing scattered like thistledown. Dilkhusha was a truly appropriate name for its owner's home for his was the happy heart of an incorrigible dreamer.

For a few weeks we had another visitor in the evenings, a middle-aged Moslem about whom we knew very little except that he had an extensive property somewhere across the field behind us. Like Farid Khan, he was a talkative man and used a great deal of florid language to say very little. He did speak more simply and genuinely about his garden and he usually arrived with a single lime or a flower which he would hand me with a deep bow.

"I have brought this for you from my orchard."

We began to find him tiresome and on one or two occasions, hearing a knock at the gate and peering round the bedroom curtain to see him standing there with his small offering, we crept quietly into the living room, pretending not to be in until he gave up and left. Then something happened to deter him forever.

One day on a visit to Miss Joseph, I noticed a small black and white puppy cowering in the grass outside the college wall. Fi had impressed on me the dangers of contact with animals and told dire stories of the horrible diseases they could spread so I hardened my heart and went past without even bending down to look closely at it and I managed to ignore it again as I went home. Then, looking out of the bedroom window, I saw a group of children throwing things at it and rushed over to drive them away. I had grabbed a towel on my way out and wrapping the poor skinny thing in this, I took it back, put it down in the courtyard and brought it some milk. It lay there trembling for a while but then got up on weedy little legs and began feebly to drink. Fi was very cross with me.

"It's not a good idea, Jo. You do realise that there's no easy access to vets or injections here and we are taking a real risk if we keep it. It's a female and that means we'll have the problem of shutting it away from other dogs every so often or we could have a whole litter of puppies to cope with at some stage."

He said quite a bit more but as a boy he had once persuaded his parents (who had said all the things that he was saying) to let him keep just such a stray mongrel. He must have been thinking of his dearly loved pet when he reluctantly agreed to let me have this one. We bathed and disinfected her and named her Shandy. Slowly she gained confidence and as she grew, became smart looking and alert.

She was a bright, responsive companion and took the edge off any loneliness I still felt. In my family we had always owned dogs and her companionship added an extra veneer of normality to my new life as well as being a daily pleasure.

Our Moslem visitor was horrified when he saw her and never called on us again. Farid Khan was both tougher and more liberal. He always insisted that we shut "that animal" in the outhouse whenever he came round to see us but he still came.

Despite joining us for coffee occasionally, Vidhya was very caught up with her Hindu friends but Celine and I often spent whole days together and it was through her that Indian news began to mean something to me. We took "The Times of India" and I did try to read it but it was a dull paper. State affairs and economic plans meant little to me and the names involved were unfamiliar, difficult to pronounce and hard to remember. I was sufficiently amused and interested when my father-in-law wrote that year to say that he had gone to bed in Bombay Province and woken up in Maharashtra to find out what exactly he meant and discovered that this one large state had been split along language lines into two – Maharashtra and Gujarat. Mostly such news was so remote from anything that concerned me that I only really spent time on the cartoons and the crosswords. At this period Goa was still a Portuguese territory but there was a growing movement to oust its colonial rulers and return it to India and Celine was anxious about her elderly parents, hoping that they would not get caught up in any trouble there. Here was a hot issue where the welfare of someone I knew was tied to dry newspaper reports and I slowly began to be interested in and understand more about current affairs.

All this time, Miss Joseph and I met regularly and we now occasionally ventured into the bazaar together in the mornings. Not waiting for Fi to take me shopping in the jeep gave me a much needed sense of independence but this came at a price. It meant sending Gopal to find a rickshaw and I really hated travelling in one of these. I could not overcome a feeling of both guilt and embarrassment every time we sat, upright and ridiculous, behind some poor man struggling to pull us along with all the strength of his spindly legs. Miss Joseph was small, delicate and elderly but I was young and strong and when we reached the railway bridge and our rickshaw-wallah stood up on the pedals to gain enough power to take us over its steep hump, I could never bear it and insisted on getting down and walking to the far side. This made both Miss Joseph and the man himself feel awkward. In a strange country it can be very difficult to do the right thing. There was so often a gulf between my ideas and those of the people whom I longed to treat with kindness. If a virtuous glow washed over me or I prided myself on being civilised and considerate, I soon realised that I was more probably humiliating these men, making them lose face and seem unable to do their job.

As April ended, this period of consolidation, in which the rhythm of my days had begun to feel more natural, took a less happy turn with the changing weather. The temperatures soared and the air became sultrier. Even inside Dilkhusha with its thick walls and shaded windows, it was becoming uncomfortable at night and we started to sleep outside in the courtyard. This had a romantic feel to start with. A cool breeze would often start up as we went to bed which brought us some relief and we could lie looking up at the stars and chatting idly. The drawback of these al fresco sleepovers was waking at the crack of dawn with the sun dazzling us and, still sleepy, having to drag our charpoys and bedding inside. We would sit for some time on the porch steps, yawning over cups of hot, strong tea, before our eyes fully opened and we could bring ourselves to get washed and dressed. Shandy was happy. Usually shut outside alone, she deserted her basket and slept under my bed.

I felt tired for most of May and June. The daytime temperature could reach over a hundred and the increasing humidity as the monsoon approached left me limp and uncomfortable. It was a real effort to go anywhere or do anything and even reading and listening to music lost their appeal. Any longings for more meaningful activities and tasks dissolved in an enervating lethargy but I was still often somewhat scratchy and irritable when Fi came home. Sometimes I was literally scratchy. Most of our washing was taken away and done by the dhobi and I tried not to think about where it was taken and what shared the water with it. Our sheets and towels were certainly fairly harsh textured after his efforts and the beatings that they received in the process made them age rather quickly. I did rinse out my more intimate garments but even so our facilities were hardly ideal and the combination of poor laundering and humidity made prickly heat a problem. The limited water we had made things more difficult. I longed for streams of cold water and instead had to make do with two or three bucketfuls. I did, though, abandon the hipbath, happy to stand and pour my ration over me.

The rains arrived at the beginning of July. We were still sleeping outside and when the first heavy shower came suddenly at about four thirty in the morning, we tumbled off our beds and dragged them into the porch, falling back to sleep on damp mattresses to the hiss and plash of rain and the feel of fresh, damp air. The next morning we woke to a different world. The porch steps led down not to a dusty courtyard but a shallow roman bath and when I went to open the gate and look out for the sweeper, I saw him wading through water towards me like a child at the seaside with his bucket and spade. The ground dried out very quickly but during a second rainstorm we were able to shower under the overflow from the roof and if it was a little muddy at first, it soon became a clear, steady flow of water that was pure bliss.

The weather had altered dramatically and our life was about to alter also. Our time in the town was coming to an end. As the monsoon really set in, we were told that our bungalows were ready and that we should move out to the factory site.

EIGHT

On the day we moved, a pickup was sent to transport our belongings and we piled into the jeep with additional packages and followed it through the usual mingled mayhem of trucks, carts, animals and pedestrians until, a mile beyond the Dairy Farm, we turned right onto a sandy track through fields of sugarcane, mustard and lentils. The factory stood on a forty acre site beside the railway line running north/south from the town. It was a plot of uncultivable soil so palely alkaline that by moonlight it looked as if it were covered with snow and so precariously anchored to the earth by thin coarse grass that any wind could pick it up and hurl it at us. The whole place was incongruous, like something from science fiction, a space station set down on an antique planet. The tall black factory chimney – visible for miles – towered above bare, starkly rectangular buildings unrelieved by any vestige of plant life. All around small men struggled daily to grow green things. At night they returned to low, rounded, dust coloured earthen houses and slept. They died too soon. In this situation it did seem as though we were an alien settlement.

If any of these thoughts struck me the day that I escaped from Dilkhusha, they were fleeting fancies lost in my sense of excitement. Just before the factory gate, between the track and the railway line, an area of about two acres had been allocated for the residential enclave and divided equally into four sections by two intersecting roadways. Each of the four identical oblong bungalows stood close to the road with the bulk of its plot wrapped around the remaining three sides of it. There was a strong resemblance to a model Toytown or Lego set, with a meticulous matching of every element. At each end of the transverse roadway was a large, high block, housing two garages below and two sets of servants' quarters above that were reached by curved stone stairways at the rear of the building. The toilets and bathrooms attached to the quarters were tucked inside these like under-stair cupboards and were basic but adequate in this context and far more generous than the limited facilities shared by the servants attached to the wealthy households in my in-laws' city building.

The rooms in the bungalows were not large but were well arranged. The living rooms – a sitting room, dining room and kitchen – were at one end of the oblong and the bedrooms and bathrooms at the other. Suddenly we had the luxury of two bathrooms! In the en-suite linked to the largest bedroom there was a shower and a bath with a large electric water heater above it. In the smaller guest bathroom there was a shower and a second water heater. A long, back verandah closed in by a concrete lattice wall acted as a passage between the two sections of the house. The kitchen was basically a galley with a small pantry at one end and a rather primitive, built-in cooking range set in a chimneyed alcove along one wall. This, like an old-fashioned copper, was made of cement faced brick. A coal fire in the body of it heated three circular openings along its top, each with a wire rack insert on which to place utensils. The architect may have looked to the West in his general plan but this was a very Eastern kitchen intended for the use of, and providing the appropriate setting for, a local cook. It was not the height of modernity but there was a waist high sink with taps and yet another water heater.

It took us about two weeks to settle in. The company had provided solid basic furniture and we decided to take our time to make any fancier additions. We unpacked our remaining crates, put our small imported electric cooker and fridge in a passage leading to the kitchen, stowed our books and records and had some pretty curtains made in the bazaar. Looking round I could almost imagine myself in a suburban bungalow at home.

Perhaps it was too much like home. I had never imagined when I first set eyes on Dilkhusha that I would ever regret leaving it but with its thick walls, its porches and deep set windows, it was built for its place in life and whatever its deficiencies, it was a refuge from the elements. Now with the benign days of winter over and heavy intermittent rain and heat to contend with, I saw it with fresh eyes. By comparison with such a venerable building, these bungalows, so immediately attractive, were pathetic toy houses, the playthings of a foreign trained architect who had forgotten the realities of his own country. Their walls were thin, their windows were unshaded, they boldly invited in the sun, the wind and the rain and the elements accepted their invitation. All through the monsoon the rain drove at us across the open fields, ran under the front door, down the hall, across the back verandah and out on the far side of the house. Luckily the monsoon in the north is not relentless and there are many dry days but we still had a frequent indoor river to contend with. There was nothing, either, to shield us from an intense sun or keep out the cold in winter. Even with a fire in the sitting room it would prove to be very chilly when the wind, following the path of the rain, blew through the house. In every season our unscreened windows faced the wide expanses of the surrounding fields and for much of the year it was too hot to close them. When we put on the lights, every insect for miles around was drawn in and our ridiculously inverted light fittings, another whim of the architect, were soon piled high with charred corpses.

Our striking gain from dealing with all this was an increase in creativity and ingenuity. Fi and I were used to very different but equally well ordered, comfortable homes and we were aiming at order and comfort here whatever the problems. We rolled up some sacks to make a set of alternating sandbags, one on and one off to dry, that we put against the door to stem the river. We tacked muslin squares over the window frames to repel the insects and turned the light fittings upside down to stop them catching those that did get in.

"Actually they look better that way. Well, less hideous anyway." Fi said.

In hot weather we cooled the house by running a perforated hosepipe from a garden tap along the eaves of the verandah to drip continuously over woven reed screens hung along the latticed wall. These screens made from a variety of Vetiver grass were called Khus Tatties and had a delicate perfume. It was a cooling system that had been in use from Mughal times but our pipe stood in for the army of servants who had continually dampened the screens for Akhbar and his court and later, the enervated sahibs and memsahibs of the Raj. The effect was achieved by evaporation and once the rains came the system ceased to work but while it did, our verandah was pleasantly shaded and a fresh, scented breeze wafted over us.

Make do and mend was our slogan but when it came to the problems outside the bungalow, no amount of personal ingenuity was any help. The forty acres of lunar landscape that we had moved onto was one of many isolated tracts of saline or alkaline soil called Oosar that are dotted all over the northern states. Even today they are the subject of ongoing experiments in reclamation. If this site, which had presumably been available for industrial use because nothing could be grown on it, was to be even minimally softened and screened, the company faced an enormous challenge. The aim was to dig out growing trenches for perimeter hedges and three feet planting holes for trees and shrubs but the tools chosen were unbelievably fragile. There were no mechanical diggers or heavy machinery, only a dozen or so villagers in dhotis and turbans with their gaunt, razor-backed donkeys and simple implements. For weeks these men dug into the ground until, reaching a hard pan about three feet down that prevented root growth, they spent hours chipping away at this with their pickaxes and spades. All day we heard the chink and thud of metal on stone as groups of diggers kept going while a thin line of men and donkeys travelled backwards and forwards along the mile long trail to a nearby village. The salty waste was carried away in panniers on the backs of the donkeys and they returned with substitute loads of the cultivable soil that had been purchased from the villagers there. We tried to stop the use of some animals.

They were all in bad condition but there were those whose backbones were breaking through skin and fur worn down by the heavy panniers. For a while the pathetic creatures were allowed to rest in the shade of our buildings but this was an unaffordable luxury. These were poor people and the men too were thin and hard working. In addition to the slog of breaking through the salt pan, they carried baskets of waste or soil on their heads as they went back and forth with the donkeys. After they left, their job done, it was a guilty relief not to have to see such things.

In that hot climate and planted in the replaced and nutritious soil, boundary hedges of acacia and bougainvillea, thorny plants meant to repel jackals and stray dogs, soon began to grow quite tall and a few shrubs made some headway. The next stage was to deal with the glaring stretches between these green islands. A dozen gardeners were taken on and they daily built small bunds or earth ramparts around sections of each plot on a rota system. These were then flooded and, after time allowed for any salts to leach out of the soil, the water was run off onto the sides of the roads through specially dug channels. We would never have a lawn but the scanty grass did take a firmer hold on these bald patches and slowly grew stronger and greener so that things looked a little less stark. Later, I even managed to grow a wide border of English flowers like delphiniums and snapdragons that flourished in the cool season but, on the sunniest days, as I knelt to weed or went to pick flowers for the house, a faint shadow of the pain it had cost always hovered over my much loved garden.

Meanwhile, as that epic daily battle with nature was still going on around us, we had a brief escape to an altogether more idyllic setting. Dr Saraswat and Vidhya got together with a group of their friends in the town to organise a day long picnic in a mango orchard about four or five miles out on the road beyond the factory. It sounded rather like a Pick Your Own arrangement by which we all had to pay the owner a fixed amount and were then free to pluck as many mangoes as we could. I had just been introduced to these luscious fruits and loved them and I was keen to go. The people from town arrived early in the morning while it was still cool and we all set off in a procession of jeeps and cars, with a number of servants, vast quantities of food and a crowd of excitable children. It was a rowdy but happy day. We set up a kind of camp under the deep shade of the mango trees, the servants took charge of the food which they set out on large white cloths on the ground and we all went off to pick mangoes. A lot of these were packed into baskets to be taken back with us but after lunch we ate too many of them. We tackled them in the Indian way, taking the mango in both hands, kneading it to loosen the flesh inside, then making a hole in the skin to suck out the juice and pulp. Quite a lot ran down our chins and the children were extremely sticky by the time all our paraphernalia was stowed in the vehicles and we set off for home.

Vidhya was clearly missing her numerous neighbours. Living out of town meant that daily contact with friends was more difficult. It was only six miles away but it wasn't an easy drive. The Saraswats and the Castelinos had their own cars but we were still dependant on factory transport. Though Fi was very busy, he always made a weekly trip to bring Miss Joseph out to spend the day with me but she and I could no longer see each other without forward planning and our easy, casual meetings were at an end. We three company wives were forced to depend on each other to a greater degree and this was as claustrophobic as I had feared. We all knew most of what was happening in each other's houses. Privacy was hard to come by. A round of inter family dinners somehow became obligatory and I came to feel that I could predict any coming table conversation to the last sentence but it was impossible to refuse invitations and then sit alone, and be observed to sit alone, in your own bungalow.

For some considerable time I was excused from hosting any of these gatherings. I was considered to be a novice, an outsider who hadn't learned to deal with servants. Gopal, our part-timer, had left us just before we left Dilkhusha and taken a full time job in the town but two weeks after our move, Fi found us a cook through one of his factory hands. Amanatullah was an elderly Moslem with a wispy goatee beard, long black garments and a generally dusty and frankly somewhat unhygienic look. This I could tolerate. My awareness of dirt was less keen than it had been. I was learning to ignore many things. I did have one real problem though. Amanatullah cooked well but he did everything so slowly that I had to clench my teeth not to scream anytime that I saw him in action or more accurately inaction. I was partially adapting to an Indian tempo but this was a stage too far. One day I saw him cycling back along the factory track from the town and I called Fi to the window.

"Look at him. It's like a circus act. The man who can ride more slowly than anyone in the world without actually stopping or falling off. It's no good. I can't get on with him. We'll have to do something."

Luckily the fourth bungalow was being set up as a guest house. There was not much work entailed and Amanatullah could produce good food so, with a helper to do the cleaning, he would make an adequate cook cum caretaker there. I could move him on to another job, clothe this as a promotion and get my way while still keeping a clear conscience. India was quickly teaching me its subtleties and roundabout techniques. Perhaps to punish me for this, we next had an unsatisfactory month with a character whom we christened Just William. We discovered that he apparently changed his name according to the religion of the family he worked for and had been variously William, Govind and Mahmud. He was also a heavy smoker and returning home unexpectedly to find him on our sofa, his feet up on the coffee table, puffing away on a cheap cigarette, we had to part with him.

Servantless again, we were wondering what to do next when we had some bad news. Don told us that he was leaving our little church. He was being transferred to Madras and replaced with an Indian padre. That night I shed a few tears. The Longs had been such a lifeline. What would I do without their down-to-earth, familiar company? It seemed that their servants were feeling equally lost. After four years with such an easy family and used to English habits they faced a difficult time. Wyn asked us if we would take them on. I already knew their little Moslem cook, Mehdi, and their general servant, Ram Singh, and I was very happy to take them both. They moved into the quarters over the garage and Mehdi brought along his young wife whom I often saw standing at the top of their stairway watching me as I worked in the garden. She always kept her face covered and if I spoke to her or if Fi came out of the house, she hastily disappeared.

It seemed wrong to have so little contact with her but to impose my ways and my freedoms on her would be as bad.

Now all my domestic problems were over. A neat, efficient, buttoned-up Moslem, a shambling, somewhat simple-minded but goodhearted Nepali and a learner English memsahib, we got on from the first and worked very happily together. It would be presumptuous to say that they liked me. It was impossible to know what our correct little Mehdi was thinking and we were all tied into a system that made completely natural reactions to one another difficult but I was very fond of them. There was a maternal element in this feeling. They largely depended on us for their care and well being and there was no escaping that – another of India's hard facts. Over the next few months, as life on the site settled into a pattern and I began to meet many of the factory staff and get to know them, I grew to like them in the same way.

NINE

The analogy with a space station extended in my mind beyond the mere appearance of the site. Managers and workers were all in different degrees aware of their good fortune in being part of an innovative project and this gave them a sense of common purpose. The managers' homes were unusually close to the workplace and the whole colony so cut off and isolated that there was a special atmosphere, friendlier and more communal than would have been likely in other factories.

Due to the company's comparatively even handed arrangements for healthcare there was also a sense not exactly of equality but certainly of self-worth among the workers. A Hindu doctor came out from the town once a week and after holding a clinic in the factory would then visit the management wives. Dr Shah was a plump, smooth-faced man always beautifully turned out, no matter what the weather, in a tweed Nehru jacket and a white congress cap. I had begun to suffer occasional stomach upsets and headaches and he had a very soothing and paternal manner.

"Don't worry, my dear. I will make you up a little carminative mixture and send it out with one of the workers tomorrow. Remember a light diet and no heating foods and two spoonfuls of the medicine after meals and all will be well."

A barber also used to come out once a month on a Sunday afternoon. Like Amanatullah, he was a Moslem clad in dusty black but he cycled somewhat more briskly up the track with his leather case tied to the handlebars of his ancient bicycle. He visited our houses in turn to cut the men's hair. The other women, with very simple straight styles and strong resilient hair, trimmed their own but mine was fine and difficult and I did not trust myself to deal with it. It was months since I had visited a hairdresser in Bombay and I was looking somewhat dishevelled, my short hair an unruly shoulder length so I made the rash decision to let him cut it. I ended up with a severe pudding basin bob, trimmed sharply into the nape of my neck and with a ruler straight fringe across my forehead that was achieved slowly, with much concentration and heavy breathing. Still it was comfortable and tidy and with a little fluffing up as I shampooed it, would serve.

The factory personnel, working in the engineering department, the laboratory, the office and on the production line, together with supplementary staff like watchmen and gardeners, totalled around ninety. There were an equal number of Hindus and Moslems and a few Christians. In the 1950's, India, possibly exhausted and sickened by the slaughter of the post-Independence era, seemed relative calm and free of sectarian trouble. Those Moslems who had felt most strongly about their rights and position now had their own country in Pakistan and had been removed from the equation. Certainly our mixed group worked cheerfully and peacefully together without strain and with no outward sign that they felt any alienation from someone of a different religion.

The Castelinos returned to Bombay shortly after the move to the site and Ozzie was replaced by a young Maharashtrian engineer called Karandikar. The men were in the habit of calling each other by their surnames but the women, for some reason, thought only of the engineers in such terms. I don't think I even knew their given names and I certainly never used them and speaking of them this way became totally natural. Karandikar's wife, Nanda, was an even more recent bride than I, having also been married immediately before coming north and this shared experience drew us quite quickly together. We were about the same age, both in our early twenties and this set us a little apart from Vidhya who was in her late thirties and already had two children.

Dr Saraswat now held another welcome party for these new arrivals. His bungalow was much smaller than the rambling house in which he had hosted ours and he decided that this one should take place at the club. In many Indian towns 'The Club' is a very colonial institution with huge rooms, bars and turbaned bearers on all sides. This was an altogether more modest affair. It was a large but simple, whitewashed building set among trees, on the road leading up to the railway bridge. We must have passed it many times on our way to the bazaar without knowing what it was. As we walked in that evening we saw that there was a badminton court immediately in front of the clubhouse, with a double row of seats set out on either side of it as if for the spectators of a match. The whole place was lit by lanterns strung on the trees and looked very festive. A bearer met us and politely but firmly sent us our separate ways. I was directed to the left and given a chair beside Vidhya and Nanda in the centre of all the women. Fi was seated beside

Dr Saraswat and Karandikar in the front of the male ranks to the right. The men were smart in dark suits and the women like a flight of butterflies in bright silk saris. It was a pleasant evening. We were served soft drinks and sweets and we all made polite conversation. What I can never forget about it is that segregation. Even the guests of honour, the bride and bridegroom, did not sit together.

Fi was now the only non-Hindu member of the senior and middle grade staff. The other men and their wives had all been brought up in, were all caught up in, a caste system that made for a rigid relationship between every strata (and every layer of every strata) of society and this meant that spontaneity and easy social interaction were difficult for them. Fi and I were lucky in not being constrained in this way.

As a Parsi, Fi stood apart from both the main religious groups with whom he worked and was therefore more easily trusted by both. This neutrality had historically been an important factor in promoting his community's prosperity and advancement under the British. Parsis had also been in the right places at the right time to attract their rulers' patronage. From the 18th century they had been leaving the rural areas and small towns of Gujarat, where they had first landed in India, and migrating to the power hub of Bombay. In every part of the country they are predominantly urban dwellers. Energetic, enterprising and educated, they are not, like many Indians, bound to specific occupations by religious taboos. Originally, rather like an Icelander, a Parsi was known by a given name followed by that of his father but in the 19th century, everyone adopted trade related surnames which give an idea of the kind of people that they are and the kind of work that they do. Some are Gujarati names: Motivala – pearl dealer; Kapadia – cloth dealer; Unwala – wool dealer; Schroff – cashier; Dubash – shipping agent. Others are English: Merchant; Paymaster; Captain; Doctor; Engineer; Contractor. There is considerable social mobility within the community and the Zoroastrian religion is essentially egalitarian in that its main focus is on individuals and their personal moral duties. An orthodox Parsi wears a special cotton vest, a Sudra, with a pocket for symbolically storing his good words, good thoughts and good deeds and these will be weighed at the day of judgement. The smallest action counts within the day to day affairs of this world and every Parsi, rich or poor, is a participant in an epic, universal battle between good and evil and contributes to its eventual outcome. This heritage gave Fi the social self-confidence to accept most people easily and without prejudice. Of course no-one could escape the inequalities of Indian life and he was not entirely free from accepted attitudes. He had been brought up with servants and there were still quite a few in the Bombay flat, but two of them had been with the family since his boyhood and they still called him "Firdaus Baba" and told him what to do.

I was used to the free and easy relationships of rural Suffolk. My aunts had cleaning ladies but there was little sense of their being inferiors and conversations between employer and employee only emphasised their equality. East Anglian farm labourers too were sturdy independent characters. There was no kowtowing there.

So for various reasons, we were both able to interact more freely than our colleagues and neighbours with everyone around us and the workers consequently felt freer with us.

After a time we got to know a great deal about them. It sounds ridiculous to say that what I felt for them was love but it was, at the very least, warm affection. They were so open, so lively and, despite all the hardships of their lives, so ready to enter with zest and eager curiosity into every situation.

I knew the gardeners, the malis, best. I was keen to work on the garden and had ideas and plans for it and I was the only person to go outside and work with them. It raised eyebrows – and the malis' hands in horror and protest – when I actually took a trowel and planted something but it was soon accepted as a foreign eccentricity like my madness in keeping a dog. They would never have heard Noel Coward's "Mad Dogs and Englishmen" but would have certainly felt in tune with it. Creating a garden, though, is a very special activity and in sharing this we came closer. Their attitude to me became one of benign tolerance. There were a dozen men assigned to this work but I knew the two head gardeners best. Sutnam, a slim, smooth-faced, soft-spoken man, was gentleness personified but his assistant, Mohan, was a tiny, wrinkled bundle of energy like an animated garden gnome in Indian dress. His immediate response to any suggestion or request was always a high toned protest.

"Mugger, Memsahib…….But Memsahib."

Mugger means "but" in Hindi and coincidentally a crocodile is a muggermuch and this was our name for Mohan.

"Go on you old muggermuch! You can do it."

I had fairly regular contact with the workmen in the Engineering Department which was responsible for general maintenance. Like all new buildings the bungalows had teething problems and one man in particular was usually sent over to deal with a loose electrical fitting, a leaking tap or some similar problem for me. Devi Singh was like the archetypal character in slapstick sketches who carries a ladder over his shoulder and turning here and there with a wide eyed, serious face causes total mayhem. It got to the point where I would stand in the doorway and bar his entrance.

"Go away Devi Singh. Tell Karandikar Sahib to send someone else."

"Memsahib, this time I am very careful. No trouble."

His anxious conciliatory smile always won me over. I had to let him in and there was often another small breakage.

Living so close to his work, Fi was never really off duty and in any emergency he was usually the manager that everyone turned to. We were once woken in the middle of the night by one of the watchmen calling loudly just outside our bedroom and suddenly a hand with a bloody thumb was thrust through the window. He had apparently injured himself on one of the gate bolts. With considerable patience, Fi brought him indoors, cleaned and bandaged his wound and sent him off with strict orders to be more careful in the future and in case of trouble to come to the door. On another night, I jumped up in fright as a head appeared through the open window above my bed, shouting excitedly.

"Sahib! Sahib! Thief! Thief!"

"Go to the door," said Fi sharply and went off to see what all the fuss was about. I followed him and stood in the hall, weak with suppressed laughter, as the man enacted a thrilling drama on our front step, with full running commentary. He leapt from one side to the other brandishing his stick. On the left, he was the thief making menacing gestures. On the right, he was himself bravely repelling the intruder. It was a lengthy fight. Finally he stood breathless and triumphant in the centre of the doorway.

"Gone, Sahib. He has run away. I have defeated."

One of the peons found a variety of reasons to call on me at home. Peon is a word with bad connotations but in India it simply means a general office worker or messenger. Har Prasad was an impressive figure, tall and upright, his khaki uniform impeccably ironed, his short hair smoothed under a Nehru cap and his white moustache carefully groomed. He had once served in the British army and later been an English teacher in a small school. I think the appeal of his present humble job was that working for this company reconnected him to the British and his memories of earlier days. He always called me "Your Honour" and his formal, even archaic English, was beautifully enunciated if sometimes idiomatically novel. He once brought me a basket of peas from his village and presented them with a deep bow.

"I have brought you these from my field, Your Honour. They are still in their youth."

From the start, he was keen to invite us to his village for Dussera. In theological terms this is a celebration of the general triumph of good over evil but such an abstract notion is embodied and made real for people in the story of how a Hindu king, Rama, defeated the demon Ravana with the help of Hanuman the monkey god and an army of monkeys. The whole complex tale is told in the epic Ramayana but there is a mini version of events called the Ramlila which the villagers were to perform as part of the festivities. Tied to the lunar calendar, the festival has a variable date but would take place early in October and we agreed that we would go. We had missed the film version of the Ramayana because of a rat. Now we had a chance to see a live version of it.

Har Prasad and a group of friends carrying torches came to escort us to his village, a mile away, across the railway line. We were warmly welcomed, seated immediately in front of the improvised stage and given cold drinks. The villagers threw themselves into action with great gusto. One combatant in a staged fight, reluctant to leave the limelight, refused to fall dead as he was intended to. His opponent kept signalling to him and hissing instructions for him to follow the script but he continued to leap around manically, waving his sword.

"Die you fool!" shouted the audience impatiently and he eventually dropped to the ground and expired with a great deal of groaning and eye rolling. The height of the drama was to be the point at which Hanuman would set light to the demon's island and destroy it. We could already see the actor in his monkey costume, sitting on the roof of one of the houses with an unlit torch and, given the wholehearted performances so far, we looked forward to this scene with some trepidation. Still, I really wanted to see it. However this was turning into a very long drawn out affair and at one thirty in the morning we gave up and insisting that we had to go home but could manage the walk alone, we stumbled sleepily back across the fields and clambered over the silent railway line. We were sorry to leave Har Prasad disappointed that we would not stay to the end but glad that we had pleased him by going. I half expected to hear the next day that the whole village had burned down but it seemed to have survived.

Shortly after this, our compound was strung with necklaces of small, flickering flames to mark Diwali. It seemed to us like a preview of Christmas. The Saraswats and the Karandikars decorated their houses, bought new clothes for themselves and gifts for their friends and for three days we all lit charming little diyas, small earthen lamps filled with oil and floating wicks, and set them out along our pathways and on our window sills.

Though we had crossed it on our walk to Har Prasad's village, the railway track on its high embankment was a line across the landscape beyond our boundary that cut us off from any view of the horizon and enclosed us even more tightly within our small enclave. By this time we hardly noticed the frequent goods trains that passed so unassertively and had lost interest in the occasional passenger train that halted at the tiny station above us and let down one or two villagers before wheezily heaving itself away from the platform and moving off towards the town. Around May or June every year, though, these trains were transformed, smothered in white clad bodies, piled on roofs, clinging to doors and windows and even sitting on the buffers between carriages. As each train began to slow down a short distance ahead of the station everyone slid down its sides and the embankment like foam sliding down a glass and flowing outwards in rippling circles. Then, as it gathered speed and moved off, the whole mass surged upwards again and roofs and carriages were once more hidden in a white froth. These were all pilgrims returning from a bathe in the Ganges that, on this special day, rid them of ten sins or even ten lifetimes of sin. Newly purified, they were all embarking on another round of transgressions and travelling without tickets.

All this sounds great fun and of course it was. Although my life was restricted to a greater degree than I had ever envisaged, there was this constant stream of novelty to engage me. But it would not be a novelty forever. This wasn't a holiday. I had to stop behaving like a tourist and become a solid resident. I had been married for ten months and Fi and I were still learning to live together. We had blithely assumed that love would leap across any cultural divide and solve every problem but love is just a four letter word as the song says and we had to define it for ourselves. If I saw the site as a space station, I could stretch the imagery to our relationship. We had taken off from a planet with a known topography and familiar customs and launched ourselves into an unknown place. Amorous astronauts you might say. We were young, inexperienced and having to overcome somewhat greater gulfs between us than many newly-weds faced and we were as boxed in within our marriage as we were within the compound, doing almost everything together. Fi did have a separate life in the factory but I had no such independent existence. This irked me and put a heavy burden on him. There were times when, overcome by boredom, I felt an urge to break out, to just walk away but, looking out over the fields around us, I knew that there was nowhere to go, no way to go. I felt helpless and imprisoned and if on such days Fi was delayed by a difficulty at work and the already endless hours stretched out longer than usual, things could get very fraught between us. One day after lunch, despite my good intentions, all my frustration burst out.

"It's impossible. I'm going crazy."

"Shush! Don't shout. The servants are still in the kitchen. They'll hear you."

"I don't care. I'll scream even if it does frighten the servants. I just don't know what I'm going to do all afternoon. I've tried everything. I put a huge effort into keeping the house comfortable. I read for hours. I'm studying seriously. I'm doing some writing. I've tried gardening. Why did I think that would work? Just look out there. The only plants that will survive this inferno are thorns."

"Calm down. You have made great progress in the garden. There are seasons everywhere. Things don't thrive all year even in England."

"Don't start on England." My voice wavered and I turned my back on him.

"Jo, let's stop this. I know how hard it is for you but we wanted this and we swore to make it work. I need you here." He came up behind me and kissed my neck.

"Don't. That's not the answer. It's alright for you. You only need me here part time. You have a job that fascinates you. You're away from the house for hours on end. How can you know what it is like?"

"Don't forget how new this project is. There are constant practical problems. I have to deal with them. That will get easier in time. Just now, I don't know what to do. I can't deal with you in this mood."

"Oh, go away! Go back to what's important to you. I don't need you here. Go and deal with your real problems. Go! Go!"

"I'm going. I can't say when I'll be back."

I went to our room for the siesta I was becoming accustomed to – a fixed set of habits seemed at such times, my only weapon against desperation – but it was too hot to lie still. The mattress forced heat upwards and the ceiling

The Civil ceremony in my in-laws flat.

During a traditional rite, my mother-in-law gives
me earings.

Badridutt, bearer and general factotum in the household,
offers congratulations.

Fi and I in formal dress for the evening reception.

Back to basics in my Dilkhusha kitchen.

Fi's daily chore: Pumping water outside the courtyard.

A horse drawn, much over-laden cart on the road to town.

Stalls in our crowded, local bazaar, our vegetable seller among them.

The factory with its tall chimney and the early trees
establishing themselves.

Fi and I outside our bungalow before any gardening work
started.

Shandy and I outside our sitting room.

Sara and I in the garden, back from Bombay and
settling down.

A proud grandfather with Sara and me outside our
latticed verandah.

Fi and Sara on one of our expeditions.

Left to right: Ram Singh, Sara and Mehdi, just before we left.

A farewell party with some of the factory staff.

fan, struggling through turgid air, was only forcing heat downwards. Furious tears had left a salty stickiness oozing from the puffed and aching swelling of my lids. Beyond the claustrophobic confines of the compound, the vast plain stretched monotonously in every direction, a potent symbol of isolation and loneliness. The servants had now gone to their quarters and Fi had walked grimly back along the dusty path to his office. He had gone such a short distance to be so far from me. I peeled myself off the bed and went through into the long, latticed verandah. The cane furniture, cleaned only that morning, was already pale with dust again. I picked up one of the faded batik cushions and hurled it across the floor and then hurled a second one after it. I wanted to break something. An act of pointless vandalism might ease the soreness and rage inside me. I stood still for a moment. What was I doing? I must get over this.

I did, but there were other tremendous fights. The problem was we always felt the need to keep the volume down. We did not want to advertise our disagreements to the whole site. In my childhood, tantrums were frowned upon and unrewarded and I had learned to tamp down anger and strong feelings, even forget them, but I could not eliminate them and, if I rarely lost my temper, when I did, it was like a volcanic eruption. Not being able to shout was a handicap and I seemed to compensate by developing destructive tendencies. This was not the only occasion on which I wanted to break things. During one bitter quarrel, I did in fact break a marble model of the Taj Mahal that someone had given us as a wedding present by flinging it onto the floor.

"Right! If you can break things so can I." Fi seized a small carved table that we had also been given and actually ripped the legs off it.

I gasped. I was stopped short and suddenly struck by the thought of Mehdi's face when he saw all this wreckage in the morning.

"Fi! We can't let Mehdi see all this. What will he think?"

We began wrapping up the debris for Fi to dispose of in the factory waste bins and, suddenly reduced to helpless laughter, saw how impossibly we had both been behaving. If things did not often end this melodramatically, they always ended quickly, for even at our most heated, we knew in our hearts that it was our situation not our true feelings that drove us to extremes. Seeing that my pent-up, unused energies needed a safety valve, Fi struggled for tolerance and patience. It helped that I was penitent, better tempered and in some measure eased for some time afterwards. Paradoxically our fights and reconciliations actually led to a strengthening of the bond between us.

There were many other ways in which we felt constrained by being constantly under observation and confined by proximity to our neighbours. It soon felt essential to get away for a while and late in October, we received a letter that gave us an excuse to go to Delhi and book into a hotel overnight. This would be our first stay there since our whistle-stop change of trains on our way up from Bombay and my first chance to really see anything of the capital.

TEN

The letter had come from Indian customs. Everyone back in England had been sent news of my wedding and I had dispatched half my wedding cake to my parents to distribute among family and friends as a sort of proof that there was no going back. I was indeed married to 'that Indian'. Unbelievably, we had been informed that there had been an unfortunate accident and that the cake had been eaten by rats at Heathrow Airport.

"What is it with rats?" I wailed. "They seem to have it in for me."

"Maybe these were two-legged rats," said Fi cynically.

We were sent a generous compensation cheque but no-one had received any cake. Still, they had all rallied and sent me gifts. These had taken months to arrive in India and months to pass through the bureaucratic system that had produced this notification of their arrival. The increasingly stringent curbs on imports meant that I was in breach of regulations. We decided that a face to face confrontation with officials might help and a visit to Delhi would also give us a chance to look for a cheap car. Having our own transport would free us of dependence on the company and make it easier for us to go into town whenever we wanted. So we travelled up by train and stayed for one night at the same small hotel as before.

In the government office, we spent over an hour on a very uncomfortable bench, waiting to see the appropriate person. He sat at a huge desk almost hidden among heaps of files and papers, busily reading and signing various items and calling on menials to fetch and carry for him. He completely ignored us. Whenever he had to look up to summon another peon, his eyes passed blankly over us as if we simply were not there.

"It's a ritual trial of strength," Fi whispered. "We'll only put his back up if we complain." This was my first experience of the petty power plays of minor bureaucrats and I was almost at screaming pitch when the officer raised his head and, as if suddenly aware of our presence, called us imperiously to his desk. He took up a fat file and looked gravely at me over it.

"This is a serious matter. These are illegal imports for which you have no licence."

"But these are presents. Wedding presents. I did not know they were coming. How could I have applied for a licence?"

Logic was of no use. The rule was that I must have a licence. I did not have one. Further argument was pointless. I decided to try a few girlish tears. Indeed I truly felt like weeping, more from an impatient anger than from grief, although somewhere deep inside there was pain. This whole episode, this pettifogging ban, illustrated quite graphically how I had raised barriers between myself and my family. It seemed like a metaphor for the divide that I had opened up. At this point Fi was asked to go through into an inner office to see a more senior man. I feel sure that some kind of financial transaction took place, perhaps a payment of a fine, or ostensibly the payment of a fine, and that it was this rather than my tears that finally freed my parcels. Anyway we were asked to return the following day to collect them. Naturally they could not be handed over without some further delay.

Before we started out for Delhi, I had pictured myself visiting proper shops and had even hoped to buy some stockings which I was told could occasionally be found in Connaught Place, an imposing circle of well-known stores in the city centre, but we actually had no time for anything beyond our business with customs and a protracted car hunt. We by-passed the shops and went behind them to an area full of small garages. We did not have a great deal of choice because of our limited budget but we finally found a second hand Ford Prefect there. It was a sit up and beg model, hardly smart or glamorous, but we finally set off for home in it, all my unopened packages a treat in store on the back seat, feeling very pleased with ourselves. We left in the early afternoon. We faced an eighty mile journey in an untried vehicle and wanted to be home before dark.

To get out of Delhi we had to cross the Jamuna River over a combined road and railway bridge that allowed only one-way traffic. We waited in a crowd of snarling scooters and roaring cars, barely restrained by lightly applied brakes from dashing into the oncoming traffic. As the lights changed, they all hurtled forward in a burst of speed and increased noise, clattered over the metal plated surface and, narrowly missing the waiting vehicles on the far side, sped off down the road ahead. We had to keep up. We felt that if we did not drive as wildly as everyone else we would simply be mown down. Gradually, though, the traffic spread out and thinned somewhat and we did slow down and start to enjoy the drive. We were after all travelling along the longest and oldest trade route in Asia. The Grand Trunk Road, running from Bengal to Afghanistan, traces its beginnings back to the third century BC. That earliest, ancient road was rebuilt in the sixteenth century by an Afghan Emperor and considerably upgraded by the British in the nineteenth and we were retracing the path of battalions of troops, of northern invaders and countless Asian traders. It was history literally unfolding in front of us.

It was also hot and dusty and the car swayed from side to side over any bumpy surfaces like a skittish pony about to kick up its heels. I could not follow the technicalities but it was something to do with its old-fashioned suspension. It *was* a small car but as huge trucks bore down on us, high, wide and apparently driven by turbaned maniacs, it felt minute. Yet, when twenty miles from home, the engine overheated and steam started to rise from the bonnet, one of those maniacs proved to be a Good Samaritan. Seeing us dithering rather helplessly on the side of the road, he pulled up and came across to us, cooled the engine with water and dampened rags and waved us off again with a beaming smile.

We had made a bad buy. Over the next few weeks we could never get from the factory into town without breaking down at least once and Fi decided that we would have to go back to Delhi to see if we could get things fixed. Rather nervously we puttered back, with several stops, and went to the same area where we had bought the car. Seeing another garage that appeared to be owned by a European, we had the racist expectation that here we would get impartial advice. We did. The owner was a large, grey haired Irishman who had clearly not kissed the blarney stone. He told us bluntly that the car was a disaster, had been in a terrible accident and had been cobbled together and held that way with a coat of paint.

"What do you think we can do?"

"Sell it to another mug if you can find one."

We did not try. We went back to the original garage and had a heated exchange with the owner that ended in his taking back the car and returning two thirds of our money. Without a car, just as the winter days were tempting us back into the countryside, Fi arranged to pay something for the private use of the factory jeep so that we could again enjoy our long, leisurely explorations.

This time we had Shandy with us. When we had first moved to the site I had been afraid that she would run off into the fields, where she might either be attacked by jackals or feel the upsurge of an inherited need for a roving life, but she never moved far away from me and even in the garden, was always close behind me wherever I went. She slept in the verandah and seemed to have no yearning for freedom but, let out of the jeep in open country, she ran round and round, barking hysterically, as if a pent up spirit of wildness had suddenly been released in her. Back at the bungalow, for some inexplicable reason, she reverted to her usual timidity and clung to my heels again.

For a short while that winter we had another companion on our outings. An administrator had been sent from Bombay to systematise office procedures and since he was about our age and was staying for only a month, head office felt that, rather than facing a solitary life in the guest house, he would be more comfortable with us. We were happy to have him. Tenduf La was quite a character, of mixed Sikkimese and English parentage, highly educated and good-looking, with a streak of mischief concealed under courtly manners. I think Fi may have had the odd jealous moment over him. On one of our picnics, we gathered the usual crowd of curious villagers who sat around at a distance openly speculating on this odd trio with its dog and concluded that our guest and I were husband and wife and that Fi was our driver. If this was a bit disconcerting, it was good for Fi to have a male companion of his own age and interests. It gave him a break from his alternating commitments to work and wife and all the attendant worries that these imposed on him. Tenduf La was very inventive in finding ways for them to pass the time together. He went off to the bazaar and bought two hookahs which he insisted that they should smoke every evening. Ram Singh, grinning widely, would bring in and light these elegant pipes for them and the two of them sat there like young sultans, puffing away at the polished mouthpieces, the water in the lower bowls bubbling away gently and the tobacco smelling faintly of fruit cake. Next, seeing two donkeys belonging to a workman grazing in the field behind us, he came up with the idea of donkey polo. The owner was paid for the use of his animals, somewhere in the bazaar they managed to find hockey sticks and using these and soft balls, they attempted a few chukkas. The donkeys were small and they were tall, so their legs practically reached the ground. They more or less walked around with the donkeys moving placidly along beneath them. They looked quite ridiculous but they enjoyed themselves and we onlookers were highly entertained. All these antics convinced Ram Singh that Tenduf La was crazy. One morning I went in to check that the guest room and bathroom were in good order and found a pile of shredded grass and plants on the floor.

"What is that Ram Singh?" I intended to suggest that he was not doing a good job of cleaning the place.

"Humko kuch malam nahi, memsahib. Wo Sahib undar lata hai. I don't know anything, memsahib. That Sahib brings it in."

As this was unlikely, I looked around more carefully and saw that some kind of bird seemed to be building a nest behind the water heater but I don't think that Ram Singh changed his mind about the culprit despite this evidence.

We were sad to lose our new friend when he returned to headquarters but soon after he left there was another distraction. Dr Saraswat dealt with both the office and the factory staff and Fi dealt with the day to day running of the production line but the manager of the Delhi office, combining two jobs, was in overall charge and had stayed on the site for one or two days at a time throughout the past year. This had brought a new face and a change of conversation to our evening gatherings that gave them a needed lift. Now, at the end of November, we had a far more important visitor.

The Managing Director came up from Bombay for three days, setting the seal on the success of the project. This was even more of an event because he brought his wife and English secretary with him. We were only fifty miles from Agra and clearly seeing this as too good an opportunity to miss, he planned to take them there during their stay. I thought that the Taj Mahal rather than the factory must, in fact, be the main attraction but I did not voice my thoughts. There were frantic preparations in the days before their arrival. Amanatullah was smartened up and given a new white coat and cap and we all sent our servants over to the guest house to help prepare the rooms and ensure that everything was in good order.

I had already met our dour northern M.D. Soon after my arrival in Bombay I had been called into his office to be quizzed on my readiness for what lay in store for me in the north. This was not because of any concern for my welfare but because he did not want Fi distracted from his job by marital problems. In those days it was not politically incorrect to openly vet company wives.

"How will you cope?" he had asked bluntly. "It's quite backward up there. The climate is good in the winter but extremely hot in summer. We'll provide a doctor but that will be a basic provision. There are unpleasant diseases to watch out for and not much in the way of modern medicine. Whole swathes of things you take for granted will be unavailable. The real problem will be the lack of the kind of entertainments and company that you are used to. It won't be easy. I hope you know what you are doing."

"I have to cope. I expect that I will."

"Humph!" He had given a very sceptical snort.

Now, his worries seemed to have been put to rest. I had lasted nearly a year without causing any trouble and during his visit he was very genial and set the seal of approval on me as well as the project. His wife and secretary were naturally sympathetic to my situation and I was invited to join them all for the day out in Agra.

Unfortunately, when we reached the Taj Mahal we found that we had come on a bad day. The Crown Prince and Princess of Japan were there as part of a tour of India and we had to wait outside in a large crowd of enthusiastic on-lookers until they had been shown round. Crown Princess Michiko had been very much in the news since her engagement and marriage to Prince Akahito in 1959. The daughter of a wealthy industrialist she was the first commoner ever to marry into the Japanese imperial family. She was considered a great beauty and noted for her smooth, pale complexion. There was much oohing and aahing as the couple came out and drove past us and we three women agreed that she was indeed very good-looking. Our escort was not so impressed and gave one of his special snorts.

"I'd rather have a bar of chocolate any day."

I don't want to make any extravagant comparisons but at a far more exalted level, this was another young woman facing the strains and stresses of breaking the rules and marrying outside the usual boundaries and she had married in the same year as I had. A decade earlier there had been similar coverage of the marriage of an English girl to an African chief. Intense political pressure, particularly from South Africa with its apartheid policy, had led to Ruth and Seretse Khama, later first president of Botswana, living in exile until the early fifties before they were able to return to his country. Such things still caused a stir and over the next years the newspapers were full of gossip about the depression and illness that the Japanese princess suffered as a result of the implacable hostility of her mother-in-law. These were fascinating media stories but I could not forget that they were also family traumas.

The Taj Mahal, an outpouring of royal love and grief sculpted in marble and decorated with a delicate tracery of flowers and flowing Arabic script, has too often been degraded to flat images on chocolate boxes and biscuit tins, just as great pieces of music have similarly been diminished by their use as advertising jingles. Yet the power of such things cannot be easily destroyed. In the clear Indian sunlight, its combined strength and fragility, so strikingly mirrored by the pale princess who had just been here, evoked as intended, thoughts of love outlasting death. It moved us all, even our gruff escort.

As a footnote to this I found Ram Singh sitting on our kitchen step one day, gazing at one of my discarded magazines. He was looking at a picture of the Crown Princess and shaking his head raptly.

"Kitni khubsurat! Kitni khubsurat!. How beautiful! How beautiful."

The morning that our visitors left, I stood watching their car, as it pulled out of the factory track and slowly disappeared along the main road. I ached with the longing to go with them. This brief contact had revived a sense of isolation and loneliness that I thought I had overcome but we soon got back into our routines. We spent most free days out and about and saw our usual friends. We had a quiet Christmas. We sadly missed the Longs. Eva and Mike were away. We invited Miss Joseph for the day and brought her back with us after morning church to share a Christmas meal, beautifully prepared by Mehdi. He had even made us a cake. I could never persuade him to use my electric cooker and it was astounding what miracles he achieved on our earthen range. He regularly made delicious bread and pastries in a tin box with a hole in the bottom that sat on one of the range openings and served as an oven. On this occasion he had somehow also managed a sugar icing and decorations. Usually straight faced and expressionless, his feelings under tight control, he even managed a smile when I praised his efforts and thanked him warmly.

I had been full of energy and happy as always in the crisp winter sunshine but in early February I began to suffer constant stomach trouble and Dr Shah's carminative mixture had no effect at all. He made several special trips out to see me and as I suddenly lost weight at such an alarming rate that I was visibly thinner within two weeks, he suggested that I should be sent to stay with my in-laws and have a proper check-up. The company paid for its employees to use one of Bombay's most modern hospitals and he felt that I needed the kind of treatment that it could offer. My poor in-laws would have to take responsibility for me again and whatever disquiet they had felt over Fi's choice of a wife and whatever reservations they had about me, we knew that they would do so. They had done their best for me when Fi first left me on their hands and they had, incredibly, provided our wedding. The Indian sense of family duty, while it can sometimes mean a loss of individual freedom, makes for a reliable support system. My English family had certainly not disowned me. We exchanged occasional somewhat stiff letters that covered the bare surface of our lives but these made for a cursory connection and my parents did not have this engrained, traditional attitude to help them overcome personal hurt and disappointment.

My relationship with my mother-in-law had become one of mutual respect and wary friendliness. From the start we had agreed that I should call her by her first name and this emphasised the neutrality of our feelings. I think she liked me as a person if not as a daughter-in-law. I was aware that I did not have the wealth or status that she had secretly hoped for in her son's wife and had joked with Fi that all I had to offer was five pounds and a fair complexion. I had read the matrimonial advertisements in the papers with their demanding standards. It was clear that the five pounds was a terrible drawback but the fair complexion was a great advantage.

Fi had now worked for over a year and was due for three weeks leave. We decided that I should go on ahead, see the doctors and that he would follow later. If I still had problems he would be there to help and if I was better, we could have a holiday and enjoy a little city life together. I was too unwell by now to travel alone by train, so Fi drove me to Delhi and I caught an evening flight to Bombay.

ELEVEN

My plane landed at Santa Cruz airport at six. I only had one suitcase and my in-laws' driver, Swami, waiting in Arrivals, waved away a clamour of porters and took it from me. As we stepped outside the airport buildings, Bombay, like a friendly but unhygienic animal, exhaled a hot, moist breath over me. By the time we reached the car my hair was already clinging damply to my neck and forehead. During the hour's drive through the suburbs into the city, the grimy, salt blackened tower blocks and wretched shanties that lined the road were already fading into the early darkness but the streets were loud, lighted and pulsating with non-stop human and animal activity.

It was a relief to reach the quiet, tree-lined, hilltop street where Fi's parents, Dara and Persis Khurody, lived. With its gardens and shaded colonial style bungalows and apartments, Carmichael Road was a calming haven from the overheated turmoil that so jolted my system and jangled my nerves and it was to remain an oasis in the high rise cacophony of the modernised city. In the early sixties, Bombay, a city squeezed between sea and sky, was on the cusp of change, about to gain much needed additional space by reaching upwards, with the first skyscraper built in 1965. This road, the home of many elite families, held on to, and still holds on to, something of the relaxed atmosphere of an earlier age of gracious living.

Darbhanga Mansions, in which my in-laws' flat was situated, was the property of a lesser Maharajah, the ruler of a small territory in Bihar, who owned homes and palaces in all the major Indian cities. It consisted of low, solid twin blocks that had been adapted to provide two spacious flats on each of four levels, all of them lavish with Minton tiled floors and stained glass windows. They had large reception rooms, three bedrooms, three attached bathrooms, wide enclosed verandas, a large kitchen and warren of pantries and servant quarters at the back.

Swami drove past the long street facade and turning into a side lane, went to the rear of the building and dropped me at the steep stone stairway that led to the entrance. He took the car and my suitcase off to the basement garages and I went through the rather gloomy hallway and got into the antiquated lift, which rattled and clanked up to the flat on the second floor. The door was opened by my favourite servant, Badridutt Misra, officially the bearer but also an emergency driver and general factotum, who had been with the family for years. He was a small, effervescent man from one of India's northern hill regions, with something of the look of a Nepali. Having a great affection for Fi, whom he had known since boyhood, he let this feeling spill over on to me and, since he spoke reasonable if broken English, had been a great support to me in difficult moments during my earlier stay.

"Joan Bai!" He beamed at me and then his face fell. "But you are sick. What Firdaus Baba done to you?"

"Badri!" I took his hands. "It's so good to see you. It's not Firdaus Baba's fault. It's India. Too many bad bugs."

My mother-in-law came out of the drawing room at that moment, welcoming but somewhat distracted. She was a neat, spare woman with a handsome face and short grey hair and at this time in the evening had changed from her daytime wear to a sari. I always found her daily transformation astonishing. In the mornings, wearing a much laundered cotton housecoat, a heavy chain holding all her household keys fixed round her waist and her hair casually combed, she was the epitome of housewifely simplicity. In the evenings, her hair severely waved, her powdered face set off by a necklace and matching earrings, a set of glass bangles on her wrist, one of her many beautiful saris worn the Parsi way, with the pallu pleated and pinned on the right shoulder, she was a slender column of extreme elegance.

"My dear girl, look at you. What is this? You are looking so pulled down. Firdaus should have sent you to us earlier. It was too bad that we did not come to meet you but Dara is very busy. He had some of his people here for a meeting earlier and I had to give them tea. He has a most important matter in hand. He will tell you all about it over dinner. I have prepared some very bland dishes. There is nothing that will upset you."

It turned out that on the twenty fourth of February, during their ongoing tour of India and Pakistan, Queen Elizabeth and Prince Philip were to visit a project that was very much my father-in-law's baby and he would be escorting them around it. He was overseeing the arrangements down to the very last detail and was completely immersed in his plans. That evening, after a brief discussion of my hospital appointments, he was very keen for me to see a copper bowl that he had in his room, made to his design to hold the soil that the Queen would use for a tree planting.

"I will let you have it after the ceremony. It will be a wonderful souvenir. Now! All the doctors at the hospital are first rate. You are going to the best place and I am sure that you will soon recover and that you will be well enough to come to Aarey on the day itself."

As Milk Commissioner for Bombay and later Dairy Development Commissioner and Joint Secretary to the Maharashtra government, my father-in-law had been responsible for a major reorganisation of milk distribution in Greater Bombay. Aarey Milk Colony, twenty miles outside the city, had been a key part of this plan. It was the largest cattle colonisation farm in Asia.

Traditionally, people had kept milk cattle, usually buffaloes, crowded into insanitary stables all over the city, with families living and sleeping on platforms above them. Fi had seen these as a boy and the memory of such squalor had darkened his face as he described it to me. As the population in the island city grew to three million, such places increased in number within already congested residential areas and in these conditions, animal health declined, many buffaloes died, milk supplies dwindled and contaminated and adulterated milk was sold at exorbitant prices. With the Aarey scheme, all these animals were removed to several special units on the new site which covered four thousand acres of land next to the National Park. This was a major upheaval within the traditional system and it did not happen without a great deal of resistance and protest but eventually the cattle owners were transferred there and were contracted to sell their milk to the government owned processing plant at its heart. Animal welfare improved, milk yields rose and clean, quality-controlled milk was distributed to families and institutions at a fair price and free to over seventy thousand poor schoolchildren.

If there were ever times when my father-in-law was difficult or high-handed (and he involved himself in quite small details of our lives, always looking for better ways to do things and sure that he had the right solution to any of our problems) it had to be remembered what he, a boy from a small central Indian city, had achieved. He had held many prestigious posts in India, done study tours of Denmark, New Zealand and Australia, been a noted participant in International Dairy Congresses and advised the Ceylon government on a Milk Scheme for Colombo. That year he was setting up a Dairy Technology Institute at the colony that would offer students a two year dairy diploma course and he was always full of ideas for ever further developments, but probably his greatest achievement was this revolutionising of Bombay's milk supply with its consequent effect on life there. Only those with a forceful personality make such an impact on their world.

Breach Candy Hospital, where I had an appointment the day after my arrival, was a curved, white building set on the seashore below the hill on which Darbhanga Mansions stood. Established in 1950, it was the height of antiseptic modernity and as far removed from Dr Shah's bazaar surgery as one could imagine. It turned out that I was suffering from one of those tropical infections that can hit European bodies hard and it was a relief to be in such a place. The white-coated doctors exuded professional confidence, treatment in a completely different league to my carminative doses was available and I would be kept under observation until it was established that there were no long term side effects from either the illness or the medication. Worries about any more serious problems were set at rest and I could plan to be among the guests for the Queen's visit.

This was naturally a memorable and exciting event for my father-in-law and his staff. For the hundred or so invitees it was very agreeable to be at a royal occasion without crowds or crushes. How it was for the Queen it would be impertinent to speculate. The facts are: this was comparatively early in her reign; India was displaying many of its most alluring aspects; in the newsreels of the time she looked animated and seemed to be enjoying it all. How inspecting buffaloes and dairy machinery compared to Jaipuri palaces and riding in a howdah at the head of a procession of gaily bedecked elephants it is again impossible to say. After she and Prince Philip had been shown round, they took tea with my father-in-law and other officials in a specially constructed gazebo in the centre of a wide lawn while we all stood rather awkwardly and uncomfortably on the side watching them. Then, with a gardener holding the copper bowl of soil and my father-in-law bending solicitously over her, the Queen planted a tree, smiled at us, waved and was gone. I have no photographs of all this. I daresay that cameras were forbidden but I did keep the planting bowl.

A few days later Fi arrived. I was feeling much better but still a little shaky and my health was a reason for us to be excused too many social occasions. When we did go to any of these, it was clear that, as Fi's wife, my status had subtly changed but I still had a sense of being an outsider. This was almost certainly my own fault. I was over-conscious of barriers that were more academic than real. Zoroastrianism in India is exclusive and does not allow converts. It is also paternalistic. The children of women like me are considered to be Parsis because of their father and are accepted into the religion while their mothers are not. Ironically, though it did not accept me, I could have accepted much of the religion. It has had a bad press! Parsis are often portrayed as fire worshippers because they always keep a sacred fire, fed with offerings of sandal wood, burning in their temples. In fact, this is purely symbolic, a reminder of the light and truth of the one God they revere. Their custom of exposing the dead to vultures in high buildings called Towers of Silence causes horrified disgust but though it is understandable and I can't shake off a similar visceral revulsion, this is hypocritical. The underground indignities of burial are equally chilling, merely hidden. For Zoroastrians, both burial and cremation involve an unacceptable pollution of the natural elements of earth, air, fire and water. This ancient belief system seems to share, and predate, the concerns of more modern movements looking to save the planet. Because the community is very concentrated, a small group marked by very clear identifying characteristics and because its survival depends on clinging to those markers, Parsi women who marry outsiders usually maintain very close ties with it but they and their children no longer count among its diminishing numbers. They do not appear to feel any less a part of it. I realised that, to some degree like them, I had rejected but was still clinging to my childhood identity while unlike them, I had no such clear or equally strong tradition to hold onto.

In fact Fi and I had inevitably retreated into the classic "we two against the world" attitude that is common to couples faced with opposition. We were able to co-exist with his family and we truly appreciated all they did for me in spite of the disappointment that I was to them but, at a deep level, we felt that we could only truly rely on each other. We were very happy to spend most of our evenings on our own, seeing films or going to concerts. Bombay had large, comfortable, air-conditioned cinemas that showed the latest English and American films and was also well served with concert halls where visiting professional musicians, high grade local amateurs and drama societies performed. It was a real culture feast.

Although he was on holiday, Fi was asked to spend one day in the company offices for a review of his work and I took the opportunity to go into town for some serious shopping, stocking up on shoes and underwear. It was a little disconcerting to buy bras from male assistants who, when told the size required, eyed my chest appraisingly. Asking to see some cotton briefs, I said that I would need something large, knowing that most garments, despite their official category, were geared to daintier Indian frames. The salesman, holding up a pair of knickers and stretching out the waistband with both hands, while his colleague pulled down the crutch, said, "Jumbo size, Memsahib." The two men looked at me with dark, velvet, innocent eyes as I wiped away tears of laughter. I still wonder if they were quite literally pulling my leg. As western clothes were largely unavailable, I bought some saris and matching material for blouses which the family tailor, hastily called to the flat, made up for me in a matter of days. I also bought two Salwar Kameez outfits, a combination of cotton trousers fitted tightly at the ankle and a long tunic which is worn with a scarf draped over the front of it and thrown back over the shoulders for modesty. I found these both flattering and comfortable.

It was sad to leave all these urban amenities but we had to go and since I was better and Fi was with me, we once again found ourselves braving Bombay Central station and boarding the Frontier Mail with our luggage and bedrolls.

The night before we left, Fi had been called into his father's room and given a stern talk on his future and the necessity for care in everything he did. He was warned not to even try to buy another car. His father knew someone who ran a fleet of company vehicles and he would try to get one of their used cars for us. His contact would ensure that it was both reasonably priced and in working order and it could be sent up to us as soon as this could be arranged.

During our first train journey, I had been tired and overwhelmed by having married in such a rush. Images of the wedding had gone round and round in my mind. Everyone in Bombay had united in warning me about the primitive nature of the place where I would be living and I had been full of anxiety about what might lie ahead of me. The whole thing had been a bit of a blur. Now I was more aware of everything around me and able to savour the experience.

Trains leaving Bombay for Delhi, pass over the sea at a point called Bassein Creek and on that first occasion I had been given a beribboned and decorated coconut to throw into the water as we passed over the bridge there, an offering to the gods and a guarantee of a safe journey. Holding this hairy thing, I had apparently also caught up one of Fi's treasured possessions. Somehow a Butler knife, a very special folding knife with a horn handle that he had owned for years, had also gone into the sea. Well, it had certainly been lost on the journey and that is what Fi believed had happened to it. This time around I made sure that my coconut was unadorned and had nothing else attached to it.

Soon after leaving the city, the countryside began to darken. My mother-in-law had insisted that I should avoid railway food and had provided us with a picnic supper, which we ate early before making up our bunks and settling down for the night. It was easy to fall asleep. The train rocked along with its monotonous, clacking, rhythmic lullaby and I drowsed off. But throughout the night there were stops at many stations. Half woken by the train's change of rhythm each time that it approached these, I was then fully roused by the bustle of passengers, the shouting and banging of doors, and slid aside the window blind and peered out into the dimly lit area outside. Even this late, there was constant activity. Porters carried bedrolls to and from the train, people greeted and said goodbye to friends and vendors walked up and down the platforms calling out in a sing song chant, "Gurum Chai! Gurum Chai! Hot tea! Hot tea!" All this time an engineer was tap-tapping away at the wheels. Lying back as the train spat and hissed before slowly heaving itself away from the platform and easing into its soothing, regular sound, I slept until the whole thing was repeated further down the line. I felt grubby and sleepy when early sunlight woke me. And it was hard to watch Fi eating his steaming, aromatic breakfast, ordered the previous evening and brought in to him on a round metal tray. I was allowed a cup of strong railway tea but was otherwise restricted to the bread and fruit that we had brought with us.

I tottered around the tiny bathroom, managed a lukewarm shower under the spitting showerhead and put on fresh clothes without feeling in any way fresher. Fi took his turn and we sat back for the hours ahead. All day we rattled through the endless, flat Indian landscape, dust and train smoke drifting in through the open window, an occasional tableau of village life appearing briefly, only to fall away behind us leaving an empty view of yet more fields. We chatted idly, half doped by the heat and the monotony. If there was a long enough stop we climbed down onto the station platform to buy a book, some chocolate, more fruit or simply to walk up and down and stretch our legs.

We reached Delhi at seven in the evening and took a taxi to our previous small hotel where we had a welcome bath, leaving a thick film of reddish dust on the water and a gruesome rim on the white porcelain. At last I had a proper meal. Rather like voyagers who suffer from land sickness after the constant motion of the sea, we felt almost giddy at first on our solid, static beds but we finally slept well until woken by a bearer with our morning tea. We went back to the station, caught a local train and were back at the bungalow by noon.

Mehdi and Ram Singh stood outside the house to welcome us, and beside them was a rapturous Shandy who had been in their care all this time. My heart, which had been sinking as we drove out of town and had really plummeted as we turned into the factory track, suddenly rose. It was surprisingly good to be back with them all.

Two weeks later this happy mood was shattered. Ram Singh came in one morning, his cheerful face dark with bad news.

"Memsahib! Sandy! Rail gari!"

He was unable to pronounce an aitch and this was his name for her. He could not go on but stood with bent head and folded hands. We knew that lately, when let out in the morning, she had taken to creeping through our thorny hedge into the field outside but she had never stayed out long. That day, possibly chasing a small animal, she had run onto the railway line and one of Har Prasad's villagers had found her lying there. All my tears were private. It was unthinkable to cry over an animal in front of people whose lives presented far harsher griefs but I was aching with guilt. Had she missed us? Had she finally taken to leaving the safety of the garden to look for us while we were away and found that new freedom enticing? Fi was worried about me.

"If you hadn't taken her in, think of the miserable life she would have had, tormented, hungry, probably worn down by litters of puppies. She had an unexpectedly good life with us."

Rational arguments have no effect on sorrow but I had to overcome it and get on with things. Yet every time that I went into the garden, I had to stop myself from calling out and waiting for an eager body to push up against the back of my legs. A combination of the sadness of this and a lingering weakness that made me particularly vulnerable to the increasing heat kept me indoors far more than usual at this time of the year. Something was needed to get me out of this mood and out of the house before the monsoon really did confine me to it.

TWELVE

In the middle of April, there was a knock at the door. There stood Badri with a huge grin. Parked in the road behind him was our promised car, a pale blue Hindustan Ambassador. The well-loved "Amby" was one of a series of adaptations of the Morris Oxford manufactured in India by Hindustan Motors. It was a sturdy and reliable vehicle, nicknamed "King of Indian Roads". It was "the" car in India, indeed virtually the only car, and it could take over a year to get one once you had ordered it. It was not at all glamorous but it had acquired an aura of glamour simply because it was used by so many powerful figures. Politicians and officials were continually seen and pictured with it on important occasions. It was an enormous step up from our decrepit Ford.

It had come up to Delhi by freight to save on the additional wear and tear of the eight hundred mile journey and Badri had travelled with it and driven it on to us. He was full of glee at having been allowed to come and intensely curious about our house and household management. I think that my in-laws, who had not yet managed to visit us, had deputed him to look us over and give them a full report. He slept in the house, spreading out his bedroll in the verandah, but he ate with the servants. He made a careful inspection of the kitchen and pantry, subjecting Mehdi and Ram Singh to a searching interrogation. The verdict was favourable.

"Good people. Ram Singh has large heart and Mehdi very clever." Badri, who was no slouch himself, clearly approved of our cook.

I was afraid that Mehdi, who was a proud man, would be offended by these questions and checks but it seemed that he saw our connection with someone who had served the family so long and who was so involved with our welfare as enhancing our status and, by association, his own and no-one could dislike Badri. He was a cheerful and lively presence and when he left after a two day stay, we were all sorry to see him go.

There was still a short time before the full heat and humidity of the pre-monsoon season hit us and we decided to celebrate our new acquisition by going to Delhi again. Fi was very busy catching up on things that had fallen behind during his leave, so we decided to go for the day. This seemed feasible given that our transport was trustworthy and we would not be spending time nursing its engine along. We were not starved for city life after our stay in Bombay, I had done all the shopping that I needed to do for some time and so we could simply enjoy our new car and the open road rather than plan anything specific once we arrived. We would have a meal in an air-conditioned restaurant, perhaps find time for a little sightseeing and that would be it.

After our original disastrous journeys, we had been told that we had missed out on an important feature of the Grand Trunk Road, the quality of roadside foods available along it. Apparently there was one particularly celebrated tea stall that sold special Indian sweets called jalebies. These were supposed to be the best in the whole area and almost worth the drive in themselves. We reached the stall about twenty miles out of town. It was a ramshackle affair with a thatched roof propped up on rickety poles, under which two rather wild looking men sat behind a bank of blackened kettles and wok-like pans on charcoal fires. We were surprised that we had missed it previously, but once we tasted the sweets, we knew that we would certainly never pass it again. Essentially, jalebis are rounds of intertwined circular tubes of wheat flour batter that are deep fried and then dipped in simmering sugar syrup that is sometimes flavoured with rosewater. Piles of these were handed to us in packets formed from dried leaves and we ate them hot and dripping, washed down by very strong tea served in small disposable clay pots. All thoughts of any interdiction on local foods were forgotten and anyway everything was so hot that it had to be safe.

We had a pleasant time in Delhi and on our way back made a short detour into the centre of one of the towns along the way where we had been told there was a pottery that we should see. In a large yard outside the sheds where the work was done, we found rows of long tables covered with blue and white bowls, jugs, vases and plates. I could not believe how cheap they were and went slightly mad, buying far too many of them. Perhaps I was accumulating possessions to compensate for other deprivations but they were a source of visual delight that gave me a continual and unalloyed pleasure.

I found the heat and humidity of the next few months especially trying that year. Although I appeared to be over my infection, I was still taking some follow-up medication that left me shaky and lethargic and I was supposed to watch my diet, which was irksome. Planning menus with the restricted ingredients available was already difficult enough and I would miss out on treats like jalebies if I were too hard on myself so I sometimes sinned, with inevitable repercussions that did nothing to improve my mood. I had been through a whole annual cycle here now and was well into my second so there was little especially new to take my attention or hold my interest.

Then, at the end of July, we were flooded. That was a rare occurrence even in this month of high rainfall and it seemed that everything was conspiring against me. Luckily the water stopped rising just as it reached our door level but all the drainage systems clogged up for a week which was unpleasant and the thought of wading through the contaminated water outside was enough to keep me indoors. There was another deterrent. The malis had a thing about snakes and had constantly warned me against them. Occasionally they would turn up in an excitable bunch and there was a lot of shouting and beating about with sticks but I had never seen the large ones that they claimed to have driven off. Now these creatures, having clearly spent most of their lives underground, suddenly emerged and were swimming all over the garden their heads raised above the water. The idea of them brushing against my legs was horrible but since they vanished again after the flood and I only ever saw them once more in a second flood two years later, it did not matter how often this threat was mentioned by the malis or my timid neighbours, I soon forgot it and continued to walk and work in the garden without fear as soon as the water had subsided.

Apart from the practical inconveniences caused by the flood, it also deprived me of company. Miss Joseph could not come on her weekly visit and I did not see anyone from the farm. I could not meet Vidhya and Nanda for our morning coffee or afternoon tea for they would not contemplate putting a foot into the floodwater and I could not overcome my own reluctance to brave even the short distance to their houses. In a way, the flood came to our rescue and gave us an excuse not to meet. Though born to the climate, they too tended to become listless in this season and we were all somewhat tired of each other's conversation. We increasingly found that we had little to say that had not been said many times already. I had brought a fresh supply of books back with me from Bombay and I turned to those. Being an intense reader, I always relied on being able to lose myself totally in a book but now even that release failed me and I found myself lying about on beds and sofas with a book in my hand, gazing vacantly at the pages. My mind seemed as stunned by the heat as my body and I could not settle to anything or force myself into any kind of creative action. It did not help that we slept fitfully and woke unrested. Even at night the ceiling fan only seemed to disperse the pooled heat above us and blow it down across our sweating bodies. Perhaps, too, my stay in Bombay had spoiled me, reminding me of all the things that I was missing out on.

Before I could become too down-hearted or impossible to live with, the rains stopped, the water drained away, the heat eased and the air dried. We started to use our Khus tatties again making the verandah a far more pleasant place to be by day and as the night temperatures dropped to the mid-seventies, it was easier to sleep well. We began to sit out until bedtime on a paved patio outside the sitting room where we had planted a kind of jasmine called Raat Ki Rani or Queen of the Night and in the warm darkness, with its strong, sweet perfume wafting over us, we felt more relaxed and comfortable, both physically and with each other, than we had for some weeks.

At this point the unexpected happened. We were told that we were to have a permanent General Manager, an Englishman from head office, who would live in what had until now been the guest house. This may sound rather an unexciting announcement but any fresh face, any added company was, by this time, something to be grateful for. The guest bungalow underwent a concerted feminine inspection by all the company wives and was pronounced fit for a bachelor. Amanatullah had gained confidence since catering for the Managing Director and looking after two important memsahibs during that important visit seemed to have jolted him into greater efficiency. If he had not exactly speeded up, he had accepted the more organised regime instituted by the able co-worker that Dr Saraswat had hired to help him.

Mr Sandys, the new Manager, arrived at the beginning of September. He was an ex-army man from a minor public school, short and stocky with a broad red face, a fearsomely upright military bearing, a sharply clipped moustache and an addiction to sport, shooting and fishing. Fi believed that it was the possibility of a free access to game and the outdoor life, together with a promotion that might have been less likely in Bombay that had persuaded him to take on this lonely job. He must often have been lonely over the next months and because I was a countrywoman and Fi shared many of his interests, he took to spending a lot of time with us. He had two shotguns and offered Fi the use of one of them if we joined him in shooting forays into the countryside.

Their main target was the ducks and geese which flocked to the small lakes dotted over the plains and once, by sheer chance, Fi shot a small deer. There will be people who are outraged by this killing of birds and animals. If they never eat a prepared chicken or animal from a butcher or supermarket (which has probably led a far less natural life than those shot this way) then I can't argue with them. What has to be remembered is that we were meat eaters and we had no access to those conventional sources that screen the brutal pre-requisite of slaughter from their carnivorous customers. I can't pretend that the two men did not enjoy the sport but we did eat, or give to someone else to eat, everything that they shot. This was a valuable addition to our food supply and every creature that we ate had a quick, clean death with no long, agonised transportation to its place of execution. All my farming relatives had a very unsentimental attitude to animals that had to some extent influenced me and now, in India, continually exposed to appalling levels of human and animal suffering, I did not find these quick deaths too distressing.

The lakes, or jheels as they were known locally, were often near villages and we frequently attracted an interested audience. The ducks, with a good sense of self-preservation, would often collect in large groups in the very centre of the water, refusing to take off. It is unlikely that they had any conception of the shame of shooting a "sitting duck" but they did sit, obstinately and for long periods. At such times the men split up and went to alternate sides of the lake and I was deputed to wade out and attempt to scare the birds into the air. On one occasion when I was less well than usual and insisted on sitting on the side-lines, Mr Sandys sent Fi off to the far shore and waded out into the water himself. He must have stepped into a deep, unsuspected hollow in the bed of the lake because suddenly he disappeared underwater and all we could see was an arm holding his shotgun high in the air like some comic version of the Lady of the Lake holding Excalibur. A roar of laughter went up from a nearby slope, where a group of villagers were sitting as if at an outdoor stage performance, and it was hard to keep a straight face as our poor manager emerged dripping from the depths, shaking himself like a terrier and sadly patting his pockets that were full of wet and unusable cartridges. Every time that we went out together there was clearly an unspoken competition going on and whenever Fi shot more ducks than he did, Mr Sandys always stopped off at our Sikh's kiosk on the way home and treated himself to a consolation prize of several bars of chocolate. That day he bought a larger quantity than usual and back at the site, disappeared indoors without inviting us in for the customary post shoot drink. The next day he was back to normal. His unfortunate accident was never spoken of and he still enjoyed our company.

There was an historic fort outside the town which had become something of a recreation area and hearing that it was possible to fish in the moat around it, he sent off to Bombay for his rods, lent one of these to Fi and took us off for a fish and fry picnic. Freshwater fish tend to have a bland and somewhat muddy taste compared to those from the sea but cooked and eaten immediately they taste good. Once we had a number of fish in our holding net, we lit a small fire in a circle of stones and impaling them on sticks, grilled them to a crisp deliciousness. As we sat there licking our slightly burned fingers and drinking the beers that we had kept cool in the water, a burly European whom we had never seen before cycled past on the other side of the moat and called across to Mr Sandys.

"I hope you enjoy the fish, you and your good wife."

Fi was apparently once again relegated to the role of driver. It was something he was learning to take with a resigned shrug. Then, as we were packing our gear in the car, the man came over and introduced himself and our relationships were clarified. We lived an insulated and isolated life out at the site with little meaningful contact with the townspeople in general. Those we did meet were usually Hindu businessmen or officials whom we met through the Saraswats. We knew that there was a university in the town but it had made little impact on us and we were only vaguely aware that it was a renowned and important Moslem institution. Suddenly through this new acquaintance we got to know more about it.

Paul Hager was a German in his late sixties, with a clear, clean-shaven face and very blue eyes. Interned by the British during the war, when he was working in Indonesia, he was one of many prisoners they had transferred to India. Here they had discovered that he was an expert in silviculture and put him to work in the Viceroy's grounds. After Independence he had stayed on in India and found himself a position with one of the minor Maharajahs and, later, had been recruited to maintain the extensive grounds of this university. Though he and Mr Sandys had been wartime enemies, they were both European men living alone and they became good friends but once he discovered that we shared his love of classical music and had an extensive record collection, he also came to our bungalow very often and he continued coming out to us long after Mr Sandys had finally returned to Bombay. Even in intense heat, he would cycle the six miles out from town, looking in his khaki shorts and solar topi like one of Noel Coward's Englishmen braving the midday sun. He was quite a character and a great storyteller with a fund of amusing anecdotes. His favourite was about his time working in Indonesia before the war. He told us that the German couples among whom he lived met in their clubhouse every Saturday to get totally drunk and that he and a bachelor friend, both relatively sober, were given the job of driving these people home and putting them to bed. They found this irksome and Paul had said, "Don't worry. I fix." He claimed that the next Saturday they deliberately mixed up the couples so that everyone woke on Sunday morning to find themselves in bed with the wrong husband or wife. That, he told us, had put an end to an onerous weekend chore.

However unbelievable we found his tales, they were entertaining and he was a great addition to our circle of friends. Through him we now met some of the University staff and their wives. One professor in particular, Dr Qasim, was a keen sportsman and frequently took part in the weekend shoots. His wife was lively, westernised and a good dinner table companion but it was impossible to imagine her trudging over sandy fields or wading into jheels as I did. Though always a mere helper and chaser of ducks, I remained the only female to go along on such outings.

As the heat and rains approached once more, these came to an end. Mr Sandys went to England for a month's leave and the Qasims left for a holiday in the hills. Even Miss Joseph, who had so far never left her lodgings in all this time, went to see her family in Kerala. I faced a tedious, uncomfortable and lonely time but I did have something to look forward to beyond the usual relief of an improved climate. Fi was already due for his second annual leave but this had been deferred until the other managers had taken theirs and we were to go away in September. His parents were very keen to see him but because he felt that I should have a wider view of India than my current alternation between small town life in the north and the cosmopolitan vibrancy of Bombay could give me, he planned to spend only a few days with them before taking me south to Ootacamund, the Queen of Hill Stations.

"We never had a honeymoon so this can be a very belated one. I don't want you to think that I don't know how to treat a wife."

With this projected break ahead, I set myself a renewed study schedule and a course of purposeful reading to get me through the heat and the rain. My spoken Hindustani had greatly improved but on the whole I was learning it as a child learns a language, through hearing and copying it, though I did have a background in Latin, French and English that enabled me to see the skeleton of the thing behind this unsophisticated daily usage. Now I sat down with my grammar and my dictionary and made an all-out effort to consolidate what I knew and build on it. My pronunciation would probably always be somewhat deficient as some of the differences in the sounds were almost too subtle for my ear. Fi patiently showed me, over and over again, how to move my tongue and lips to achieve the right effect but, though I always made myself understood, I probably never quite sounded entirely authentic. In Bombay, I had bought a History of India, some books of Indian short stories and one or two novels by Indian writers which I aimed to finish before my holiday. If I occasionally found myself drowsy and slow witted, I rinsed my face in cold water, sat under the fan and pushed myself on. I stayed positive and active. Time did not drag as badly as I had feared and the day of our departure came round more quickly than I had expected. Once again, at the beginning of September, we boarded the Frontier Mail for Bombay knowing that this time we were only on the first lap of a longer journey south, with the exciting thought of a new and, for me, unexplored India ahead of us.

THIRTEEN

As Fi was with me, a more ceremonial greeting awaited us than when I had come to Bombay alone. Even his father, who despite his short stature always imposed himself on his surroundings and collected a hovering crowd of deferential officials around him, was there to dignify our arrival. Persis, standing at his side, looked me over critically.

"You are looking well again. Perhaps a little too full in the face and you are losing your slim waist. Better not put on too much weight."

I had grown used to such frank appraisals, to sitting among family groups who freely discussed my appearance among themselves as if I were not there. I had even learned to cope with public enquiries over my bowel movements, a topic of concern in a climate that often caused malfunctions. There was no reticence in such matters. As we did the rounds of family and friends and underwent this kind of scrutiny and grilling, it seemed that aunts and cousins had also noticed a change in me.

"You are looking quite plump. Is there any good news?"

Once you were married, the question of children was immediately on people's minds and quite openly on their lips. Strangers on trains (thankfully uninterested in your "motions") would go through a series of questions on your job, your salary, your marital status and the number of your children. If you had none, they wanted to know why and hoped that you would have "good news" soon.

I knew from the increasing tightness of my carefully laundered dresses that I did need to watch myself or, with the unavailability of replacements, I would find myself with little to wear but I decided to enjoy my holiday before taking action. Our family duty done, we went off to catch yet another train and spread ourselves comfortably in our compartment for the twenty eight hours it would take to reach Madras. This was only the beginning of the long haul to Ootacamund and we had a reunion to look forward to at this first stopover. We were meeting the Longs and staying the night and the following day with them. Seeing them on the station platform as our train drew in, I felt a rush of affection and it was good to spend time with them but also surprisingly sad. They had begun to talk about people and places unfamiliar to us and when we spoke of those we had in common from our earlier time together, they displayed a hint of detachment. This was their present and that was their past.

Living in India, with its transient expatriate population and a mobile elite moving restlessly across the fixed solidity of indigenous life, we were already becoming accustomed to making many friends but also to losing them. Our friendships were like hothouse plants, quick-growing, bright, cheering but fast-fading. We would always remember people with warmth and try to keep in touch with them. Sometimes, as now, we would meet them again but between such meetings would lie separate, unknown lives that had changed us all. There would always be shared memories to hold us in each other's minds but no continuing, shared history to bind us tightly. We would miss such friends and be sorry to say goodbye to them but we would learn to let them go. We were young and we never imagined being old or living in a cold climate where people are literally more shut in on themselves and social contacts provide a poorer soil, in which friendship is slow to germinate. We did not know how lonely our memories of lost friends might one day make us feel.

When we said goodbye to the Longs the next evening, we had arranged to see them again on our way back but we forgot them easily. Our minds were on the fascinating journey ahead of us. Ootacamund or Ooty, as it is known, is situated in the Nilgiris or Blue Mountains in Tamil Nadu and we were catching the overnight train to the town of Mettupalyam, a hub for road, rail and trade links into the hills. We never actually saw the town itself because we arrived there very early the next morning and, still sleepy, gathered our things together and simply walked across the platform to find some hot tea and snacks before boarding our final train for a four hour ride on the Nilgiri Mountain Railway. This is one of the steepest tracks in Asia, passing through sixteen tunnels, over two hundred and fifty bridges and round one hundred and eight sharp curves. Once again, as on the Grand Trunk Road, history unrolled before us. The British, busily establishing hill stations and extending their influence in the mountainous areas of both the South and North, had started work on this line in 1894 and extended it as far as Ooty in 1908. I only learned all these facts later. I was not thinking of such things that day. We were only half awake as we stumbled along to our first class carriage at the front of the train. Then, as it started to climb, so slowly that we felt that we might get out and walk alongside it without ever getting left behind, the air grew progressively cooler and damper and our eyes finally opened fully.

The tiny engine panted through a rolling, grassy landscape dotted with stone cottages, passing stations with names like Hillgrove and Runnymede and we could almost imagine that we were travelling through one of the neatly beautiful counties of England but when it stopped at several small halts to take on water and the passengers clambered down to get refreshments, the hubbub on the station platform reminded us where we were. We hung out of the window taking in the higher, more exotic expanses of tea and bamboo plantations and waving to the passengers in the rear carriages, when, on the sharpest bends, the train almost doubled back on itself bringing them really close to us. Each time that we crossed one of the high, track-wide bridges over a deep gorge and I looked straight down into the depth, it appeared that we were suspended in mid-air with no apparent support. I had to move back into the carriage, take a deep breath and even close my eyes, feeling slightly giddy. In the tunnels with acrid smoke forced into the carriage, I did actually feel sick. This was not helped by a continual jarring rattle under the carriage floor that occasionally made me almost lose my balance.

"It's a specially designed cog on the train catching a toothed rail that runs along the centre of the track." Fi, with his interest in all things mechanical, had been reading up on this and explained that it was what was called a rack and pinion system designed to hold trains firmly on narrow, mountain lines and get them up steep slopes. It was a special feature of this particular line and has always excited train buffs.

We arrived in Ooty just before midday. To compensate for our hasty wedding and railway honeymoon, Fi had booked a room in the Savoy, an old and noted hotel set in wooded grounds above the town and I found myself once again living in colonial style luxury. Every morning we emerged after an enormous breakfast, to become complete and unashamed tourists. This was the last month of the monsoon and there were frequent heavy showers but enough dry days for us to walk everywhere. We strolled along leafy roads between neat cottages and villas with names like Windermere and The Haven, set in idyllic gardens full of stocks and delphiniums and roses. We spent a day wandering round the extensive and beautifully laid out Botanical Gardens and visited the impressive nineteenth century St Stephen's church with its beautiful stained glass and huge pillars that, we were told, had been brought there by elephants. We went down to the renowned boating lake and hired a rowing boat for a gentler form of exercise and I was astonished to see punts there that had been made by Salter Brothers of Oxford. It seemed incredible that they had come from so far away. Had they travelled uphill on the roof of that toy-town mountain train? Perhaps the more likely but less exciting explanation was that Salters had sent men out to make them on the spot. Reluctant to abandon a mental picture of a small train chugging painfully up its steep track, laden with punts or indeed another, as intriguing, of elephants helping to build a church, I didn't ask for the details that might have been so much more mundane than my imaginings.

It was hard to believe that we were still in India. Of course Ooty was a creation of the British. In the time of the Raj, it had served as a summer capital to the Madras Government and there had been cricket and polo matches, point to point races and gymkhanas, kennels and stables. It had even been possible to ride to hounds with the Ooty hunt. This had been a resort for countless English people for years and some of them had stayed on here after Independence, finding it a perfect compromise between their colonial lifestyle and a familiar environment. The place was such a concentrate of a certain way of life that it was more English than England. We were in a theme park, an idealised mini version of England, set down in the hills of India. It was charming but it had an unfortunate effect on me. I was horrified to find myself occasionally shaky with a threatened onset of tears. I couldn't cry. It would be cruel when Fi was so delighted to have brought me here. I wondered rather wildly if the rain was working some kind of sympathetic magic on my tear glands but there was a more probable explanation. All this greenery, this rain and these country cottages were making me homesick. As an antidote to this, I persuaded Fi to travel a little further afield, to places a little less evocative and emotive.

Doddabetta, at over 8000 feet, the highest peak in the Nilgiris, was about six miles out of town and the fact that we went there by taxi as if taking a trip out into suburbia seemed symbolic. The British had found a gentler, tamer India in these hills and moulded it in their image. The vehicle was well cared for but ancient and the driver felt it was unequal to the final steep incline up to the viewpoint. We trudged up and gazed out over the wide vista of small forest areas and grassland, with the hills rolling away into the distance, enchanted but somewhat breathless after our climb.

Our other excursion beyond the town was to a settlement of the Toda tribe. This whole area had once been tribal land owned by several small, peacefully co-existent groups. The Todas were the highest ranking among them and it was they who, having sold acres of their holdings to the English at a knock-down price and making possible the whole Ooty phenomenon, had then found themselves reduced to a modern tourist attraction. There are probably no more than a thousand of them left in their small communes and today there is an ongoing effort to preserve their way of life, with the lands they inhabit under consideration as a UNESCO World Heritage Site. A Toda hut must feature in thousands of holiday photographs and was something that we were told we must see. Built of bamboo, with a thatched roof that curved down to the ground and an inset frontage of dressed stone, it looked like a combination of a Nissan hut and a gypsy caravan taken off its wheels. With painted, symbolic designs on its stone facade and a low entrance, more like a cat flap than a doorway, it was picturesque but probably very uncomfortable. This tribe, traditionally traders in dairy produce, believed that the first creation of the gods, before the first man and the first woman (who like Eve was made from the man's rib) was the sacred buffalo. The person of highest status among them was the Holy Milkman, a priest who cared for this animal. I could see amusing parallels with my new family. Fi's paternal grandfather had run a dairy business in central India that supplied the military. He and his father were following a family tradition. Both were dairy graduates working in the same field and I think there might have been an element of dynastic coercion when Fi chose his career. I have been known to joke that I made a big mistake when, instead of marrying an oil Sheikh, I married a milk Sheikh and though I grew very fond of my father-in-law, after our holiday, whenever he was at his most imperious, I took a secret delight in thinking of him as the Holy Milkman.

All this time we had avoided the town centre but on our last day we went shopping. We were looking for small gifts to take back and for something a little different as a souvenir and we found a bookshop. It was not Foyles. It was only a narrow, dusty corridor with shelves on both sides but I had a nostalgic half hour there and came out with a bag of books and Fi was amazed and delighted to find a copy of "Enrico Caruso", a biography of the singer written by his wife Dorothy. This was certainly an extraordinary memento of an Indian hill station.

On our upward journey, the train had huffed and puffed its way along the steep track, clinging to its pinion rail in order not to slide backwards. It took far less time to get back down the hill but there was still another overnight journey back to Madras, where we stayed with the Longs again. In the morning, they came to wave us on our way back to Bombay and as the train gathered speed, we saw them grow smaller and smaller behind us as if warning us that they were disappearing from our life. Not long after this Don died of cancer and Wyn went home to England and we never saw them again.

After a further two days with the family in Darbhanga Mansions, we travelled back to Delhi on the Frontier Mail. This was becoming more of a routine than an adventure. We were developing the insouciance of commuters and we were no longer held by the immense panorama of India spread out beyond our carriage window. Waking in the night to the noisy urgency of people who had somehow materialised out of that quiet emptiness in a collective spasm of intense activity, we simply yawned, turned over on our bunks and went back to sleep.

FOURTEEN

After we came.......... I am fighting a visceral reluctance to write 'home.' Our bungalow was the place where we lived, the place where we lived together and yet everything in me resisted describing it as home. Since my dramatic departure from England this word seemed to have disappeared from my vocabulary. If I used it at all, it was to speak of my childhood in East Anglia and then I was speaking not so much about a place as a perception. I wondered if it would ever be a word that I could use naturally again.

So let me put it this way...... After we came back from our holiday, it was not long before there were signs that my weepiness had probably been caused not by homesickness but by hormones and that I might well have some good news for the family. At the end of November, feeling that Dr Shah might not be able to deal with this during one of his calls at the house, which were always more social than professional, I went to see him in his surgery. That was rather a grandiose misnomer for his small, ground floor room in the heart of the bazaar. Outside the building, a vendor had spread cheap saris on the ground and the two or three that he had hung from a string across the window were all that gave patients any privacy.

"When did you last have a normal monthly show?" the doctor asked with his head bent and his hands busily tidying papers on the table in front of him.

"In the middle of October but it wasn't quite normal."

"Well my dear," he raised his eyes and looked at me, suddenly brisk and business-like, "you need to be examined but this is not a matter for me. I will arrange for you to see one of our lady doctors at the hospital."

This was a relief as I did not trust the saris, fluttering in any light breeze or sudden draught from a passing vehicle but I have to say that I did not find the hospital very reassuring either.

It was a stark, grimy building among tattered trees at the far side of the town. The room that Fi and I were ushered into had depressingly dark, unpainted cement walls and did not look totally antiseptic. Three women in rather grubby, crumpled cotton saris, whom I took to be ancillary staff but who turned out to be doctors, were sitting behind battered wooden desks. One of them took me through into a smaller, equally dingy room where there was a threadbare examination couch. On a plain wooden table beside this, was a chipped, enamel washing-up bowl with a pair of rubber gloves floating in it. The best I could say for this arrangement was that it was a step up from my Dilkhusha kitchen. I climbed up onto the couch and tried valiantly to think of England but it was no use. My whole body was revolting against the place and continually clenched in on itself. The doctor finally gave up in exasperation and said that as far as she had been able to tell, I was pregnant but that I was making it very difficult for her and that she would speak to Dr Shah about me. Fi decided that I needed the reassurance of something more akin to Breach Candy and arranged for me to see a gynaecologist in Delhi. There it was finally confirmed that I was indeed pregnant and that, based on the dates I had given, the baby was due in July.

After that I was on my own and life went on as before. Dr Shah, who had made it clear that this was a feminine business and "not a matter for him", came to see me still but only to enquire in a very general way if all was well. I have never had a baby in England so it is hard to make comparisons but I have, in recent years, heard and read a lot in the media about the dangers and difficulties of reproduction. In keeping with a general hysteria about what we should eat, how far we should walk, how long we should sleep and what supplements we should be taking in order to survive as long as possible, a mother-to-be is subjected to a prescriptive regime of supervision, tests and advice that, while it may keep her healthy and save her child from dire consequences, must also put considerable mental strain on the poor thing. I lived in happy ignorance. I went out with the men as usual all through the winter and they did not hesitate to ask me to wade out and deal with the ducks or, when it was stuck in sand, to help them push the car. I ate with a good appetite and I slept well. I met all my friends as before and no-one was particularly worried over me. I did seem to be ballooning at an alarming rate. Persis sent me two maternity dresses that her tailor had made from his record of my measurements but as these were more like tents with fitted shoulders, I took to wearing the more forgiving and endlessly adjustable saris that I had.

With Agra just fifty miles away and more quickly accessible than Delhi, Fi and I had occasionally driven over, not to see the sights but to eat out, do a little shopping and enjoy a slightly upgraded environment. The Karandikars had never been and had not yet seen the Taj Mahal. Nanda was unhappy to have missed such a chance, so, in early January, thinking that a diversion would be good for me, Fi suggested that we should all go for the day. In a photograph taken that day, Karandikar, Nanda and I will stand together in front of the Taj forever, smiling broadly. I am wearing one of my maternity dresses, white cotton patterned with small dark flowers and, with my bump, I look like a small cupola that has fallen off the building. I also look extremely well. When I think back to the nonchalant way that we breezed through my pregnancy, I can only be grateful that I stayed that way throughout. Perhaps the fact that no fuss was made over me and that I was just expected to carry on was actually good for me.

In February, Mr Sandys was posted back to Bombay and Dr Saraswat took over his role. This meant promotion for Fi and a change of title. As Assistant Manager he would get an increase in salary and an additional week of annual leave but, with minor additions, his work, the day to day overseeing of the production process, would remain essentially the same. Karandikar was also promoted and after a transitional three months in which he would train a new man to take over his position at the factory, was to be transferred to headquarters. The trainee engineer, Pathak, was a Punjabi and soon after his arrival, a third engineer, a South Indian called Srinivasan joined the department. He was a specialist, on a temporary posting to oversee the installation of some new equipment. Morning coffee sessions were enlivened by two new faces, Pathak's young wife, a sweet girl, aptly nicknamed Billo or

Kitten, and Sita Srinivasan, a smart and sophisticated thirty year old. Suddenly we had something new to talk about, new lives and opinions to explore.

Our small community had suddenly become more diverse which was interesting in the light of a long standing national controversy that had reignited in these last months. In 1950, the Indian Constitution had decreed that Hindi would be the country's official language, though it had allowed a transitional period up to 1965 in which English would continue to be used. Even before Independence there had been violent agitations over this question. The non-Hindi speaking southern states felt at a disadvantage and bullied by those whom they designated northern Hindi Imperialists. In hindsight, their determination to hold on to English and their continuing use of it in education actually gave them something of an advantage, when, much later, offshore work poured from the West into India and China. It was, however, a long running and very divisive issue and in 1963, it had certainly not been resolved. As recently as January, Nehru had introduced an Official Languages Act to allow the continued use of English after 1965 but, at the same time, Hindi had been made obligatory in all central government offices. Supporters of Hindi had waged an 'Angrezi Hatao' or 'English Out' agitation in 1957 and now another fierce campaign against English in any form was being fought by a political party called the Jana Sangh. We were hearing reports that their members were painting out English road names and signs in Delhi and other cities.

At any of our dinner parties, we presented a picture of the problem in microcosm. Among us were those who variously spoke Hindi, Punjabi, Marathi, Tamil, Gujarati and English. Fi's official mother tongue was Gujarati though he mainly spoke English – as they all did. In Darbhanga Mansions, I had constantly seen linguistic diversity at work. I have heard Fi's father address a question to his mother in English, only to hear her reply in Gujarati and that too a very idiosyncratic Parsi version of the language. Meanwhile the family spoke Hindi when dealing with the servants who, in turn, were mainly Marathi speakers using Hindi as a lingua franca. Badri's original language would have been an obscure hill dialect that was unknown to everyone. This was a home in which three languages were often used within the same conversation. There were times when two or more languages were used in the same sentence. Such a free for all would have made discussions between all of us on the site meaningless. As we debated this very up-to-date topic and I tried to sit neutrally on the side-lines, feeling proper colonial guilt, it was impossible not to point out that we could not have discussed it at all if we had not used English.

We were isolated but with more people moving in and out of the factory we were not cut off from such news and we kept up an interest in current affairs. We also shared more frivolous moments. One day in March, we were all chasing each other around the houses, flinging coloured powder everywhere and shooting bright liquid at each other from cheap water pistols. Looking like a bunch of crazy clowns, our faces and clothes a multi-coloured mess, we collapsed in helpless laughter and it was hard to believe we were ever capable of serious-mindedness. This was Holi and the whole country had regressed to childhood. We were doing so at the invitation of the Saraswats. They had provided all our colours and paraphernalia and, after we had cleaned ourselves up, treated us to another of their delicious vegetarian meals.

In April, Nanda decided that since she and Karandikar were going back to Bombay at the end of June anyway, she would leave sometime in May and stay with her family to avoid part of the coming heat and discomfort. I was also planning to go to Bombay at around that time. I had refused point-blank to consider our local maternity ward for my delivery but Delhi was too far for any sudden last minute dash to a hospital and if I spent the last two months of my pregnancy with my in-laws, I would be able to see a doctor at Breach Candy before having the baby there. I could also get my teeth checked for the first time since leaving England and finally do some shopping for baby clothes and other necessities. There was very little that I wanted to buy in our bazaar and so far all I had were a few things I had been given. Secretly daunted by the thought of an eight hundred mile train journey alone, I was relieved when it was arranged that Nanda and I should travel together. I wondered how she really felt about it but she was politely agreeable and showed no sign of worrying about my condition.

One person who did show some anxiety was Miss Joseph, who was upset to think that I had to spend so much time away from Fi and all my friends just when I might need them most and when it was already bad enough that I would not have my mother with me when the baby was born.

"I know just how lonely it can be when you are ill and far from home and family and this is so much more."

She became quite sentimental. I could not tell her that the harsh truth was that my mother might be less than delighted at my news. In the battle over my marriage she had once used unpleasant words to describe children of mixed race and though I knew her propensity for saying a great deal

154

more than she sometimes meant and was sure that her heart would win out over her prejudice in the face of an actual grandchild, this was not something I could easily forget or forgive. Nor was it something that I ever spoke about – not even to Fi. A week later, Miss Joseph came out for the day with a small parcel, beautifully wrapped in tissue paper and tied with gold ribbon. Inside was a delicate, cobwebby baby cardigan and bonnet that she had made herself. It was the only pretty thing ready for this baby so far and I hugged her with tears in my eyes. She was such a friend, such a gentle, good soul and her life seemed so hard. I thought of her at those times when she had probably been ill and alone and I could have sobbed on her shoulder. I was getting rather sentimental too.

On the twenty first of May, with Fi booked to come to Bombay in July for the birth, I was off to Delhi once again to catch the Frontier Mail. Nanda and I made ourselves comfortable in our small space. This time I was allowed to order railway food so we had fewer packages to find room for and avoided uncomfortable picnics that scattered crumbs and food particles everywhere. The porters brought us hot food, nicely laid out on trays, and took away all the debris afterwards. There was no way that I could even attempt to cope with the bathroom. It had always seemed impossibly tiny and now I felt two sizes larger and my balance wasn't so good. I brought along some cotton wool and two bottles of eau de cologne that would have to substitute for bathing. Somehow I managed. Nanda retired tactfully for her shower, leaving me to it in the darkened compartment. I would be quite pleased to see my in-laws on Bombay station but I was even keener to see the comfortable bedroom and large bathroom that awaited me in their flat. Washing and water do tend to become something of an obsession in a hot, humid climate.

Both families were awaiting us and there was a bit of a melee at the station, with introductions all round before we separated and went our different ways. I was sad to see Nanda go, wondering if and when I might see her again. I would miss her. Persis was somewhat shocked by my appearance.

"My dear girl, are you having twins? You are very large. We must get you to the doctor as soon as possible."

FIFTEEN

Once again I had arrived just as there was to be yet another of my father-in-law's Aarey events. A new hostel for dairy students had been donated by the New Zealand Government and it was to be officially opened in three days' time, on May 25th. There was no question of my attending the ceremony but the rest of the family would be turning out in force. Despite this other preoccupation, Persis gave me a great deal of attention. She was genuinely concerned about me. I was, after all, about to produce her first grandchild and she made it very clear that so far I had been taking the whole thing much too casually. I had not seen any doctor, I had taken no especial care of myself, had in fact been racketing about the countryside, getting brown and ruining my fair skin and I had absolutely nothing in the way of clothes or equipment ready for this important child. She had already done more than I had and both bought a few things and gathered others in from the family. She alternated between scolding and spoiling me. She insisted that the following day I should take a complete rest after my journey before beginning my round of dental and medical appointments and then going off with her for a mammoth shopping spree. I was given a light supper, had the longed for bath and was sent early to bed.

I had been told to rest but, though I did not expect privacy and was resigned to the fact that none of the inner doors was ever shut, I had forgotten just how unrestful the flat could actually be. I might often feel lonely in my factory bungalow but there I had all the privacy and peace I could wish for. I was used to waking at about seven thirty when Mehdi knocked gently on our door and came in with a tea tray. While Fi bathed and dressed, I would lie in bed, sipping tea and slowly surfacing into the daylight. It was always very quiet in the compound outside and both Ram Singh and Mehdi moved barefooted and silently about the house. We never had breakfast before eight and I could take as long as I liked after that to get myself fully dressed and ready to start the day. Here, Persis always got up at five thirty and immediately created an audible bustle about the place. On my first morning, I could hear her giving shrill orders in the kitchen, rattling her keys and unlocking the mesh-walled pantry in the corner of it, to dole out the day's ration of rice, lentils, sugar and tea to the cook. Servants were already moving furniture and swishing besoms around the living rooms, muttering to each other and clanking the buckets of soapy water they used to wash the floors. I had been given a back bedroom and its window overlooked an enclosed courtyard in the centre of the building. A hum of activity rose from the servants' quarters below and since all the flats opened onto this space, the neighbours could also be heard getting ready for their day. The morning sounds from Indian bathrooms are quite disconcerting. Everyone gargles and spits with enthusiasm and has an endless, varied repertoire of throat clearing routines that suggest a daily attempt to regurgitate the pollutants of an unclean city. It was hot and I couldn't bury myself under bedclothes. The only thing to do was to surrender and get up. So I wandered sleepily into the verandah and sat there flipping through papers and magazines and lifting my feet for the servant to sweep and wash the floor around me. Suddenly my father-in-law erupted from his room, immaculate in a cloud of eau-de-cologne. It was an apocalyptic moment, the advent of a deity, and as he marched briskly down the hall, there was a hushed silence, all the domestic activity ended and the servants vanished.

We sat down to breakfast and Badri, hastily buttoned into a white tunic, brought fruit, tea and toast to the table and hovered behind us waiting for our orders for eggs. Persis ate little. Her attention was focussed on her husband, who was full of the coming opening but also concerned with a more immediate matter. Nearly every Indian religious group marks the successful completion of the seventh month of pregnancy with rituals involving sweets and he was keen to send some to all their family and friends announcing that I had reached this milestone. The previous evening he had been to his favourite sweetshop and brought back a quantity of silver boxes filled with a somewhat suggestively shaped confection specially made for this purpose. He handed Persis a list of names and instructed her to get the parcels delivered as quickly as possible before dealing with a number of other tasks related to the hostel ceremony. He had written these down for her also. Sending me off to my pre-arranged dental appointment that morning, she was more than a little harassed.

"Swami can take you in the car but he has to deliver these sweets and then go on to Aarey to pick up Dara. You will have to come back by taxi. What to do? Thank God, you are so capable and sensible. You are used to managing things alone."

I climbed a shallow flight of stairs to the dental clinic, becoming unexpectedly breathless. The dentist looked a little taken aback when he saw me and when I had lowered myself into the chair and he tilted it backwards, if he did not exactly recoil, he was clearly shocked at what he saw in front of him or rather perhaps in front of me.

"Are you sure that you feel well enough for this, Mrs Khurody? Perhaps we should leave your treatment till after the baby is born."

"No. I'm fine. There are still two months to go and this is something that needs to be done."

As I stepped out onto the street afterwards, the scalding air practically blasted me back into the building. The Bombay climate is never really comfortable. It is always humid, with a salty edge to its humidity that erodes metal and irritates skin. Now, in the pre-monsoon season, the temperature was around ninety and the humidity nearly eighty. I looked around me rather desperately. Every road in Bombay normally buzzes with swarms of black and yellow taxis and as soon as you stand still on the edge of a pavement, even if only waiting to cross the road, one will pull up beside you like an importunate wasp but I could not see one anywhere. Cars, scooters, rickshaws and trucks hurtled past in the usual suicidal free-for-all but there was not one bright roof among them. The owner of a shop beyond the entrance to the clinic, who had been standing in his doorway all this time, came across to me.

"Madam, the news came on the radio. Our wonderful Taxi-wallahs are on strike again. There will be no taxis till after midnight. Please go back inside. It is too hot just now."

Perhaps the heat was affecting my ability to think clearly or perhaps I dreaded facing the dentist's obvious reluctance to take responsibility for me but I made the rash decision to walk. It was probably just over a mile back to Carmichael Road. I had forgotten that it was all uphill and I thought that if I went slowly, I could manage it. I set off determinedly but the fierce heat was almost liquefying the pavement and it felt like trying to walk through water. My clothes were soon soggy with sweat, my skin clammy and sticky, my skirt clinging to my thighs like clutching hands, further hampering movement. My chest grew tight, threatening a reflux of childish tears. I stood for a moment, wondering how I was going to find the will to go forward. Just then, a taxi did pull up beside me and the driver looking furtively around, leaned out and asked in a low voice where I was going. Told that I needed to get to Carmichael Road, he said he was going home but that he would pass the end of it on his way.

"Juldi, Memsahib! Quickly, Memsahib. Sit in front. Sit low. I take you."

He was clearly nervous and must have believed that sitting beside him, I would look less like a passenger to a casual glance. When he dropped me at the corner of the road, I went to take out my purse but he said, "No money. On strike," salaamed and shot away before I could protest. I was in such a state that I did not take the taxi number and had not asked his name. I had not paid him and I had no idea who he was. What he had done might not seem much but he could have suffered badly if he had been marked as a strike breaker and it was an act of true generosity and humanity. I have never forgotten it.

The next morning I woke with uncomfortable cramps in my lower back and discovered that I was bleeding slightly. It was the day of the hostel opening and I did not want to worry Persis but I was frightened and had to tell her. Consulted over the phone, the doctor said that given the physical strain that I had undergone, the best immediate treatment was rest. I should lie down with my feet raised and come in to see him as soon as possible the next day. If there was any deterioration in my condition then I should call and he would come over to see me. My father-in-law had gone out to Aarey very early and Persis left to join him about mid-morning. As she went out she was still anxiously talking to Badri over her shoulder, telling him not to leave me until she returned and to give me light food and whatever drinks I needed. I sent him off to make me tea and cried a little. I wanted Fi. I felt uncared for, alone and bereft and I was scared that I had done some irreparable harm to my baby but by the time that everyone came back in the early evening, my long rest seemed to have worked and the pains had stopped. The next morning I was absolutely alright again and knowing that I would soon see the doctor, much happier.

Persis, relieved that I was much improved and feeling that things were no longer urgent, insisted that I should continue to lie down for the rest of the day and not overstrain myself. She arranged for us to see the doctor in the early evening but just before we were ready to leave, I alarmed everyone and terrified myself by going into labour and we rushed to the hospital ahead of time. I was hurried into a consulting room and once the doctor had examined me he was very angry.

"What on earth have you been doing? What was your doctor in Delhi doing? This isn't a premature birth. This is a full term baby."

Though we had almost forgotten about it, this was the eve of my birthday and apparently I was going to get an extraordinary present. I felt pain but I have no real recollection of what it was like. It is an abstract memory. Eventually the pains were quite strong but once in the delivery room, I felt, if not exactly relaxed, safe, and everything went surprisingly easily. The doctor, his anger over, kept jokingly telling me to hold on so that the baby and I could share our special day but there was no holding her back and she arrived shortly before midnight.

"The next time that you do this, you had better come to see me a little sooner." The doctor again took a severe tone with me. "We must all be grateful that everything has gone so well."

Unbelievably, Fi came panting down the corridor just as I was being taken back to my room. Apparently, getting a call from his father, he had done a dash to Delhi airport. He had covered over eighty miles in an astonishing hour and a half, driving as recklessly as any truck driver and terrifying the poor man who had gone with him in order to take the car back. Dr Saraswat had phoned ahead and booked him a seat on a late flight and after landing he had found a taxi driver who, hearing why he needed to be at the hospital, had put a foot on the accelerator and a hand on the horn and got him there in record time. Back in my room, telling me this, he sat close beside me holding my hand tightly. The horrifying realisation that I could have given birth on a train or a Bombay pavement had badly shaken him and still overshadowed his relief and happiness. I was euphoric, on a high, and could not stop talking. The baby lay peacefully in a cot beside us, dressed in something that Persis had brought in. I had imagined all new-borns as red and wrinkled and I was astonished at how pretty she was. She was pale and smooth with huge dark eyes and a fluff of dark curls. Having gloated over their granddaughter, the in-laws went home and the nurses left us alone for a while before the baby was taken away and I was told that I must try to sleep. Fi was sent off with orders to collect some baby clothes and nappies and not to come back without them.

The next day brought me down. I appeared to have little milk and the first feeding times were tense, with an agitated mother and a furious red-faced baby. After several miserable attempts, a sensible nurse decreed that this must stop, that breastfeeding did no good if it was so fraught and Fi was sent out for bottles and baby formula. I was told very firmly that I must not give in to feelings of inadequacy, that I was doing the right thing and I could at last lie back and enjoy holding the warm, contented baby asleep against my shoulder.

We had decided to call her Sara. I loved the name and spelt that way it would be appropriate in any context. It would not mark her out specifically anywhere. As a gesture to my family we also called her Margaret after my sister. Fi had cabled them the news and they had sent congratulations, demands for further details and a tart comment that I apparently could not be counted on to do anything in an orthodox manner. Many of the Khurodys' friends, phoning Persis to thank her for the seventh month sweets only to be told that the baby had already arrived, seemed to share this opinion.

Two days after I left hospital, Fi had to go back to work. I wanted to go with him but still reeling from the near disastrous result of the shortcomings of our local medical facilities and worried about my travelling so soon, he insisted that I should stay in reach of a decent doctor and the hospital for at least another month.

It was a four week ordeal. Persis seemed to have regressed from modernity to some earlier age where all the baby lore of her ancestors held sway. She began by asking how I would bath the baby – the Parsi or the English way. The Parsi way apparently involved sitting on the floor and holding the baby on my knees while soaping it vigorously and stretching and massaging its limbs. I opted for the English way. When I wanted to close my door and keep my room quiet while Sara was sleeping, she said that I should not fuss and that the old custom had been to bang saucepan lids near a baby to accustom it to noise from the start. I still closed the door. Her other two obsessions were discipline and the dangers of overfeeding. She was adamant that to pick up a crying baby was to train it to be demanding and to give it more than a basic ration of food was to risk damaging its digestion. Here I hesitated. This baby didn't merely cry, she roared. She had very healthy lungs and a healthy appetite and appeared to be continually hungry. I was almost sure that I should be giving her more milk but I was in terror of doing the wrong thing. Every instinct urged me in one direction but awareness of my ignorance left me torn in the face of the certainties and determination of an older woman who had already raised two children. I knew that she was not bent on harassing me but only concerned for the wellbeing of her granddaughter and she was, after all, the person that I temporarily depended on for everything. Fretted by all these worries and conflicting theories while at the same time entertaining a constant stream of visitors and well-wishers, I was anxious and exhausted most of the time. It was a huge relief when, at the end of June, my father-in-law, delighted to be a grandparent but probably dismayed by all the attendant disruption, told me about the wife of one of his business contacts, who had also come to Breach Candy Hospital to have her baby. She was returning to Delhi by train the following week and would be very glad of my company on the journey. We would share the usual two berth compartment on the Frontier Mail and her brother, who would accompany us to deal with any difficulties, would travel in an adjoining coupe.

India is huge but wherever we went, north or south, Fi's family knew someone, or knew someone who knew someone, ready to welcome us, help us, drive us about and even accommodate us, always with genuine warmth and friendliness. It was sociability on a grand scale and cured me forever of the awkward wariness that is often the English reaction to strangers.

We met Mrs Singh and her brother, who were Sikhs, for the first time on the station platform but, within an hour, she and I were sitting opposite each other in our mobile nursery, surrounded by carrycots and baby gear, bathed in the milky, powdery scent of small infants and she was calling me "beti" which means daughter. She was a plump, placid woman in her early forties. This was not her first child. She had two older boys who had been left with their father and ayah in Delhi and she clearly regarded me as extremely young and inexperienced. She treated her large, turbaned brother in a similarly maternal manner. He seemed devoted to her. He took the overflow of our luggage into his compartment and was continually fetching this or that for her, getting out at stations to bring us tea or dealing with the food trays left from the meals that the porters brought us, even taking away for disposal the unpleasant packages that we handed him after dealing with the babies' toilet, errands which he carried out with endless patience and with the calm dignity that I always associate with Sikhs. Even seeing him in the corridor the next morning, bending over to comb out his incredibly long, thick hair did not detract from this. Enclosed in our confined space, with a willing go-between to deal with the outside world, Mrs Singh and I slept in short snatches, fed and cuddled the babies and gossiped lazily. We took little notice of the hustle on station platforms and barely glanced at the vast Indian countryside rolling past our window. Once we all parted at Delhi station, I did not meet them again but for twenty eight hours they were as close to me as anyone I had known for years.

As the train pulled in, Mrs Singh's husband had been waiting at the edge of the platform and Fi was walking alongside the carriage with two porters already engaged to transfer my luggage to the car. With Mr Singh and his large brother-in-law, Fi and two sets of porters coming and going, it was very confused and crowded in the compartment for a while and there was a good deal of shouting but eventually we all stood on the platform for a brief exchange of thanks and goodbyes before plunging into the anarchic mob blocking our way to the exit. Holding Sara close, bent protectively over her, I could not make my usual energetic push for a pathway through the blind insistence of the crowd and it took some time to get out of the station but once we had reached the car, Fi stashed everything with speedy efficiency and we drove off through Delhi's evening haze, negotiated the Jamuna bridge and its snarl of traffic and were at last out of the city. Fi drove very carefully along the darkened road and it took us two and a half hours to reach the site. Sara who had been fed on the train slept all the way.

SIXTEEN

Spending my first weeks as a new mother in someone else's home, my every tentative move subject to scrutiny and criticism, had been wearing and as we drew up at the bungalow and Mehdi and Ram Singh, beaming broadly, rushed out to help us with all our gear, a surge of relief and optimism washed through me. It was short lived. It was all very well to have escaped my mother-in-law's advice and admonitions but I had left behind modernity, medical facilities that I trusted and any credible source of support. It hurt that Fi had missed out on the first weeks of his daughter's life and that we had not shared such a special experience. It was good to be back with him and consoling to share my worries with someone who totally shared my responsibilities but he knew even less about childcare than I did.

The day after my return, the Baby Austin bounced along the road towards us and turning into the compound came to a stop against the garage door.

"Do you know what this man has done?" Eva climbed out holding an untidy parcel. "Run out of petrol! He's still running out of petrol after all these years. But don't think that it was romantic. I sat for ages in the car while he walked back to the farm to get a can. We're lucky to be here. You're lucky to be here. What have you been doing? I know that everyone does things in a hurry in England but this was crazy. You frightened poor Fi to death you know. You look tired, Joan. Are you going to get an ayah? I think you should. They deal with everything and all that milk seems to pass right through a baby. It's a non-stop job. Now let's see this one. I've got a present for her."

Eva cooed and chattered and Mike made suitable noises but I saw that I would not be looking to them for advice. I was once more overcome with terror and guilt. I knew nothing. I had recklessly brought a helpless child to this outpost. What if Sara became really ill? What would I do?

Miss Joseph was my next visitor and obviously no expert either but she was, as always, sensible and consoling and helped me to overcome this panic.

"My dear, I believe that babies are tough little creatures. Look what many of them survive in this country. Look at what you have both survived so far. If there ever were an emergency you could be in Delhi within two hours. But look at this sweet little thing. So healthy. So contented. You are so very fortunate. Stop worrying. Be happy and enjoy her."

I calmed down. I was lucky. She *was* a happy, healthy baby and, apart from a colicky hour or so every evening, slept well, and ate well. Slowly my fears subsided. I began to relax and do what my instincts told me.

There were still problems. It was the hottest and wettest month of the year. Fi had asked a local carpenter to make a cot, had decorated it himself with animal transfers and placed it under the ceiling fan in our third bedroom. We poured water onto the tiled floor around it in the hope that with the fan blowing down, this would cool things a little but power failures were a day to day reality and there were many times when we waited, sweating and uncomfortable, for the standby factory generators to start up. I also worried about leaving Sara alone at the other end of the house. The latticed verandah that was our only passageway between living rooms and bedrooms had made me jumpy ever since we had first moved in. I had never admitted to concerns about bandits but knowing that they were far from mythical and having heard further stories about their depredations in other places, there was a residue of apprehension somewhere deep inside me. Whenever I had gone across to the bathroom in the evening, I had been conscious of a huge, darkened space outside the open-work wall and felt exposed and vulnerable. This was I knew a completely visceral and irrational fear but often a jackal would howl quite close to the house and that weird, haunting sound had always made me scuttle for the safety of the sitting room and Fi's company. Once we had a solid and much higher hedge between us and this alien wildness, I had felt a little easier but now my anxieties revived and I made frequent checks on the baby and began to go to bed unusually early to have an excuse to be near her.

We were suffering the plague of insects that was always so much worse in the monsoon season and I had to turn off the light in Sara's room and keep a decoy light on outside it whenever I fed or changed her, in the same way as we had always managed meals in the dining room. Fi decided that we had put up with this inconvenience for too long and that it was time to repeat an often refused request for mesh screens to be fitted to our windows. Our old Managing Director had recently retired and his replacement, known as a difficult man, wrote back vetoing screens and saying it was no hardship to eat without lights. He had often eaten in the dark, in restaurants all over Europe and paid exorbitant prices for the privilege. Fi was wrestling with his many anxieties, finding fatherhood weighing on him and, uncharacteristically touchy, he was very upset by this frivolity. He made the rash decision to retaliate and nearly lost his job as a result. Responsible for our factory contribution to the monthly company magazine, he sent off a totally black photograph with the caption: 'Factory staff enjoying a dinner in the dark. From left to right…' The M.D. was furious. Perhaps the heat of India can do dangerous things to people's minds. He said that Fi had made a laughing stock of him and that such disrespect warranted dismissal. Cooler directors intervened. He eventually had the grace to admit that his letter had been provocative and Fi was saved. Not only that but we were granted our screens.

The monsoon, as always, passed. With a raft of baby things in the boot and Sara in a carry cot on the back seat, we resumed our usual outings into the countryside. If he wanted to do any serious shooting, Fi went out with Dr Qasim and one of our Moslem workers but even on these family outings, he carried his gun in the car. One afternoon as we crossed one of the wide canals that ran through the fields, he noticed a flight of ducks coming down on the land side of the inspection road running alongside it. He pulled up beside the gate that closed this off and saw that the chain on it could be easily opened. He gave me a look, took some tools from the car and started to undo it.

"No Fi. You can't. We'll be in trouble."

In the 1870's, fifty eight million people in India had been affected by successive droughts. Official bungling and a lack of railways to transport food to areas of need had led to many deaths. Then, as seems to have often happened, a British failure galvanised British enterprise and an accelerated programme of railway building and irrigation schemes was set in motion. By the 1890's, an additional ten million acres of land had been made fit for cultivation, watered by a huge system of canals on which an eighth of the population depended. We were aware of some of these facts and very aware that these waterways were incredibly important and constantly maintained and that the inspection roads were strictly closed to all but canal officials and workers.

"See! I've opened it. There's no-one around. We can just drive a short way, see where those ducks are and then come back. There'll be no harm done."

There was a streak of anarchy in Fi that always shocked me in someone so apparently conventional and law abiding but it was useless to argue when he had one of these reckless moments. It was not an exciting ride. The road was straight and smooth, the water on one side was calm and still and the fields on the other flat and dry but after about a mile Fi saw the ducks on a small pool among those fields and got out of the car with his gun, startling the birds into flight. As they flew over us, he shot one but it did not fall immediately. It fluttered some way and dropped to the ground on the other side of the canal.

"That was a stupid thing to do so near the water." He leaned his gun against the car. "I can't leave it. It might be injured."

Before I could protest, he had stripped to his underpants, dived in and swum across the canal. I could see him hopping around barefooted in the crop on the far side. He swam back triumphantly with his duck and stood next to the car grinning and shaking himself like a wet retriever. I sat in silent disapproval as he wiped himself down and pulled his trousers on over his wet pants. We drove back along the canal without speaking. He carefully reassembled the chain and closed the gate behind us.

Two weeks later, just as we were finishing our lunch, two policemen arrived in a jeep and arrested him. Dr Saraswat came out from his house, still holding a chappati in his hand, to see Fi in handcuffs and me standing at the door begging to be told what was happening. Apparently we had been seen on the canal road and our car number taken. Where on earth had the witness been? I had seen no-one for miles around. We persuaded the police to remove the handcuffs and the jeep went off with Fi in the back. Dr Saraswat, telling me not to worry, that he would sort things out, drove off behind them in his car. Of course things were sorted out and within two hours he brought Fi back. Payments had been made and charges dropped. Soon after this, in true Indian style, Fi was sent a permit to use all the canal roads whenever he wanted to.

After getting safely through the early weeks after my return without any emergencies, I had slipped back into our little world as if floating out into a warm pool. If it had its limitations it also offered security. It seemed the nearest thing to home that I could hope for. For most of Sara's first year I was in a sort of dreamy, maternal haze. I had entire days of happiness, quite a large part of them spent feeding her. She had a huge appetite and quickly grew plumper and prettier. On sunny winter mornings I usually put her out in the garden, in a second-hand pram that Fi had somehow, somewhere found for me. Ram Singh would go out to check on her at regular intervals and the malis, suddenly very busy in our plot, frequently stopped to talk to her. Devi Singh, still being sent to carry out minor repairs in all the bungalows, always came over to waggle a finger at her. Har Prasad made a formal call on us to offer his congratulations. I was a memsahib and a foreigner with some rather peculiar ways but they had grown used to those. I had been here with them from the start and they saw me as one of their own.

Healthy as she was, once she reached her first birthday, Sara had to be vaccinated. Smallpox was still a serious threat. Immunisation programmes were only just being developed and were far from universal but they were available even here and we had to steel ourselves and take her to the local hospital. As we drove into the grounds and parked under some scrubby trees, a small Muslim in what I was coming to regard as the regulation dusty black, came up to the car.

"Sahib, Memsahib. Doctor told me you were coming. No need to enter hospital. Better, more cleanly, outside. I have all necessary equipments."

From the pocket of his long coat, he drew out a discoloured tobacco tin and opened it to reveal a vial and a sort of tiny, metal wheel inside. I realised with horror that he was actually not a porter. He was about to carry out the vaccination himself and with this unhygienic apparatus.

"Come on, Jo. It has to be done. I'm sure things are not as bad as they look and it's all that's on offer." Fi looked a little grim but his voice was steady.

We already knew that the vaccine was not given by injection but by scratching the skin with some kind of instrument before applying it, a method that would leave a permanent, circular scar, and we had decided to have this done on Sara's leg to avoid disfiguring her arm. I held her with her skirt raised, my eyes closed, and when it was over, I was pale and shaken but she was smiling and unbothered throughout.

Looking at Sara and feeling the fierce protectiveness she evoked, I was at last beginning to understand how hard my defection had been for my parents. At the time, blinded by my own hurt and later far away from everyone associated with it, I had largely put them out of my mind. I had written only intermittent, dry, little missives that were more like official reports than genuine communication and these letters were a tiresome chore. I could not mention anything without having to insert a paragraph of explanation or description: "You remember Miss Joseph. She is the elderly teacher that I told you about, the Christian from Kerala." "You remember Badri. He is the Khurody's old servant who helped me so much when I stayed with them." I was talking about people and places that meant nothing to them and I was not sure that letters or even photographs could ever bring India to life for them in any meaningful way. The birth of a grandchild however, immediately changed things for all of us. I had to overcome the inertia induced by the seemingly irreducible emotional distance between us and find a way back to them and a more natural way to talk to them. We were dealing with both mental and physical distance. Flights were costly but it was more probably a total inability to imagine themselves in this alien place that prevented them from ever considering coming out to see us. Now they pressed me to bring Sara to England.

Two months after her first birthday, just as the monsoon was really setting in, I left Fi behind again and boarded a flight for London en route for my former home in Oxford.

INTERLUDE

I will pass very briefly over my stay in England. India was by now where my life was centred and it is that life that I am trying bring alive again. England was both familiar and strange and even though it was August, felt cold. There was the usual mix of cloudy days, showery days and even warm days. It was actually quite good not to know what each one would be like. Long seasons of unchanging days can be monotonous and this edgy unpredictability had its good side. It kept us alert and flexible. If it rained today, it might well be hot and sunny tomorrow. Still, the highest reading, of 77 degrees, only just topped our lowest winter day-time temperatures. When most people were walking about in cotton frocks, I continually needed a cardigan. This was not the only coldness. Having grown used to the exuberant openness of Indians, I found all these quiet people, with their shuttered faces, unexpectedly disconcerting. I was full of vivid impressions of my adopted country, longing to talk about the extraordinary places that I had been and the colourful people that I had met. No-one was particularly interested. After a short, polite silence, they moved on to more familiar matters. I was glad to see my parents and my sister's family. Sara had two young cousins who spoiled her and I knew that it was right for her to get to know them.

Everyone lavished love and attention on her but they hardly mentioned her father. We had achieved an apparent reconciliation but the past was dead, no-one here had come to terms with my present or my future and the pain we had inflicted on each other would always linger in some corner of our minds, blurring all softer, kinder memories. We had a week's holiday with my parents at the seaside. We visited all my relations in Suffolk. Strangely, their reticence did not feel odd. I could not imagine them anything other than cool and laconic. Back in Oxford for a final fortnight, I did a lot of shopping; buying gifts, replenishing my wardrobe, and stocking up on toddler outfits for the coming year. I left at the beginning of September, promising another visit but I did not ever consider a permanent return.

SEVENTEEN

At Delhi airport, the warmth of a late evening wrapped itself round me like a comfort blanket. There were no shuttered faces here. A fringe of smiling, waving people hung perilously over the rails along the roof of the terminal. Inside the building, they fell on the emerging passengers like rugby players fighting for a ball. Porters hovered on the edges of these mini scrums like urgent, helpless referees. There was much exuberant hugging, some tearfulness and, as the new arrivals emerged for air swathed in orange and white garlands, a great deal of shouting, with everyone giving contradictory orders in all directions. Fi, so often left behind but always waiting patiently at stations and airports, stood on one side, calm and quiet as an Englishman. As he held Sara close, he gave me a look over her head that said as much as all the noisy wordiness around us.

That winter, after a long avoidance of our outpost, people suddenly wanted to stay with us. Sara seemed to be a greater attraction than the Taj Mahal. Fi's father, who had always had frequent meetings in Delhi, now suddenly found time and a driver to come over for several weekend visits. He rearranged the furniture in his bedroom, told Mehdi and Ram Singh how they should do their chores, went around the garden with the malis suggesting various improvements, took endless photographs of his granddaughter, posing beside her, beaming with pride and after looking round the factory and giving Fi pointers on how things could be better done there, disappeared down the road in a cloud of dust.

In January, Persis came for a fortnight accompanied by one of Fi's distant cousins who was on his way back from Bombay to the small town in central India where many of my father-in-law's relatives still lived. Having made a detour to see that she arrived safely, he stayed on for her first week. He was a sweet, gentle man and spent a lot of time playing games with Sara. I had been slightly wary about having my mother-in-law but she seemed happy with the way that I ran the house, was quite impressed by both the servants and abandoned any worries about Sara, a sturdy toddler who was clearly healthy, happy and unspoilt. This quiet time together in our contained, unhurried world where she was free of the burdens of her Bombay life and the demands of a somewhat exacting husband, brought us much closer.

Our bleak plot had by now been transformed into something more like a garden and, in the clear winter sunshine, enclosed by a thick hedge, it was an ideal playground for a small child. We fixed up a paddling pool and a covered sandpit outside the verandah and I would sit in the sun with a book while Sara paddled and sploshed contentedly beside me. Perhaps because she was surrounded by an indulgent but understated attentiveness from all our work people and could always count on their patience and affection, she was an undemanding child, often totally absorbed in her own little world until, suddenly, she would run off after the malis and I could hear them murmuring away to her as they let her help them in some of their garden tasks. She also had a surrogate grandmother in Miss Joseph who, ever a teacher, encouraged her in creative activities. They spent hours sitting on the floor in the verandah, their bent heads touching over a wooden jigsaw or an alphabet game.

Maybe Fi had been more concerned about the unsettling effects of my trip to England than I had realised and wanted to give me something to ease my return. For whatever reason, he went against all his own dire warnings over Shandy and returned one day from a solitary work related trip to Delhi with a small golden cocker spaniel. He said that it would be good for Sara to have a pet and this puppy had been given whatever injections were available. Not only did we have another dog, we gave her another alcoholic name. We called her Sherry.

At about the time that I had left for Bombay, Mehdi's wife had also gone off to her family in a distant village, and we had both returned with babies. Her son, Ali, was a month younger than Sara and when he too started walking, he came into the garden most days to play with her. Mehdi seemed very happy about this even though Sherry was a third, and from his perspective less agreeable, member of this small playgroup. If there was an occasional spat, the two children generally shared a small tricycle and various other toys peaceably and took little notice of the puppy gambolling around them.

As the heat once again slowly increased and the sunlight became more painful than pleasant, we spent much of our time indoors. We could still go into the garden in the early evening but, by day, we were mostly confined to our screened verandah. It was always cool and dim there but, one morning, just as we settled down, it suddenly grew really dark and we could hear a terrifying, rushing sound outside. Going into the sitting room, I saw a huge, high column of dust whirling towards us over the fields. I ran to shut the windows but I was too late. They were torn from my hands and smashed against the already closed screens. Glass forced through the metal mesh fell in shattered globules on the floor. It was frightening and dangerous and I caught Sara in my arms and fled into the windowless passage between a bedroom and bathroom. We stood there until the rush and roar of the wind died away. There was an eerie silence. It was still very black outside and peering into the thick murk, I realised that the car was no longer standing in front of the garage and I could just make out the shape of it in our neighbour's garden. Our plants and hedges, having fought to establish themselves in harsh conditions, were tough and, though rather ragged, had suffered little real damage but the trees along the main road had been flattened, some falling to the right and others to the left as the whirlwind passed. A metal framework recently put up as the skeleton of a new factory warehouse had been bent double and bins, boxes and building materials had been scattered everywhere. It took some time to move the car and several days to restore order but by that evening the air was still and calm again.

I had long ago come to terms with a less domesticated country than the one I was born in and its intrinsic harshness had, until now, been as much a source of rather illicit excitement as disquiet. I had been coping with extremes of weather long enough to take them for granted but this was my first actual experience of the destructive potential of the climate and it left me shaken. Suddenly I seemed less casual, less able to deal with or dismiss difficulties and not long after this storm, I faced a situation that further unsettled me.

I had never been happy about the jackals that occasionally howled in the field between us and the railway line and I knew that numbers of wild dogs also roamed about there but had come to rely on the barricade of our thorny hedges and to feel quite safe inside them. Then, one day, there was a huge outcry as one of these dogs was seen in the compound, dripping drool from its mouth and almost certainly rabid. Fi was called out to shoot it and one of the factory sweepers took it away and burned it but the fear of infection remained and now we felt the folly of keeping a pet. Though none of us, including Sherry, was thought to have had any kind of contact with the animal, we were at sufficient risk to warrant our having anti-rabies treatment. This was a terrible procedure involving daily injections in the stomach for fourteen consecutive days. These had to be administered at the hospital which, despite its dingy appearance and our doubts about its hygiene, was the only place where the vaccines were considered to be kept in proper conditions. Once more we found ourselves back under the trees there, in the centre of a kindly intentioned but obtrusive crowd, drawn by the drama of the whole thing. We were by now resigned to al fresco clinics and lack of privacy and bravely exposed our stomachs to the public gaze and when Sara was given her jab, I was somehow unsurprised to see our Sikh stall keeper bending solicitously over her and holding her hand. Later that day, Fi and Dr Saraswat met the town's Medical Officer and persuaded him that, since our factory laboratory had the appropriate facilities to store vaccines, it was safe to hand these over to them and allow our doctor to come out to the site and administer them each day. So every morning we all lined up in our verandah in front of Dr Shah. We feared that we would lose Sherry but as she had been inoculated as a puppy, we were advised that giving her a similar course of injections would be a sufficient precaution and she was saved.

Facing this awful threat and its painful treatment in these backward conditions was frightening but when on the second day Sara had a fever and Dr Shah voiced concerns over the possibility of a one in a million chance of an adverse reaction, fear turned to absolute panic. It was not spelled out for me but I gained the distinct impression that in these cases the vaccine could actually result in rabies. For the only time in my life, I was literally unable to stand. My legs were boneless with terror. Luckily, within two days, her fever came down and she was clearly alright. We had survived another danger more or less unscathed though, by the end of our fortnight, there was hardly an inch of space between the hard, red lumps on Sara's small stomach in which to insert a needle and we were all extremely uncomfortable, icepacks doing little to relieve either the throbbing or the subsequent, persistent irritation of these excruciating and unsightly scars.

We were not directly prompted by this crisis, the tornado or any other specific cause but such events clearly stirred us, woke us from an almost torpid, unquestioning sense of belonging in this place. Though we had been prepared to face the consequences of the decisions that had led us here, we had to think again about involving an innocent child in our difficulties. That we had inevitably done so in a broader way and already, somewhere inside, felt a degree of guilt over this, made us keen to take charge of those things that we had the power to change. We grew increasingly aware that it was necessary to move on. Fi also began to think of advancement in his working life and I was emerging from my maternal cloudland. Motherhood was satisfying but I still had unused abilities and all my earlier frustrations lived on. Fi needed fresh challenges, I needed fresh company and mental stimulation and we had Sara's future to think of. There were simply no acceptable educational or recreational facilities for her here. Fi began looking out for new opportunities in his field knowing that it would take time to find anything that improved upon his current position. He did not want to rush into anything.

Before we went ahead with another extreme change in our lives, we decided to have a short holiday, our first as a family, and to drive up into the hills. We felt that a change of scene would distance us from our familiar routines and allow us to see our way ahead more dispassionately. We decided to visit Musssoorie, four hundred miles or so to the north of our town and, like Ooty, a popular hill station. On our way up there we would pass through Dehradun, a pleasant town in the foothills, lying between the Jamuna and Ganges rivers, a staging post for train travellers who find buses and taxis there to take them on the last few miles of their trip into the mountains. More importantly for us, it was also the setting of Doon School where Fi had been a boarder from the age of ten. He had never put it into words but I was aware that, though he had not been actively unhappy there and had been physically well cared for and intellectually stimulated, it had, like all such schools, sometimes seemed a lonely place and had encouraged in him the sturdy independence and self-sufficiency that was both a blessing and occasionally a bane in our life together. He had told me so much about his time there that I was keen to see the place and get a more definite picture of this important part of his life.

On this journey, as always, there was someone within the family's web of acquaintances to offer us overnight hospitality and we stayed with a Sikh dairy farmer, in his large, comfortable house on the edge of the town. He proudly displayed his herd of Jersey cows, beautiful and, in that setting, exotic and gave us glasses of freshly drawn milk, so delicious that milk has never tasted quite the same again.

Replete with a sumptuous breakfast and this ambrosial drink, we set off for a tour of the school campus. As we drew up in front of Fi's old hall of residence, an elderly man in a worn, khaki uniform came round the corner of the building, clearly curious to see who had driven up.

"Good Lord!" Fi sounded amazed. That's someone I recognise. He was here during my time."

There was an animated conversation in Hindi which I only partly followed and suddenly the man laughed and turning to me, spoke in English.

"Memsahib, I was knowing your husband. Very quiet boy." He turned to Fi. "But I am thinking you too, one of those rascals stealing my chicken."

Fi laughed and told me that a group of his classmates had indeed once raided the servant quarter compound and stolen a chicken and badly cooked it over a camp fire behind the school.

"It was an awful thing to do but we were very young and wanted an adventure and we were also sometimes left hungry after a poor school meal."

After a brief tour of the building, vacant at this hour as all the boys were in classes, Fi passed some notes to his guide saying it was payment for the long lost chicken and after a warm goodbye we set off for the steep climb into the hills.

Mussoorie was almost seven thousand feet up in the mountains, with spectacular views of snow-capped peaks behind it and the Doon valley and lower hill ranges stretching out below. Though it too owed its existence to the British, it was altogether more rugged and more Indian in character and atmosphere than Ooty. Once again we stayed at a Savoy Hotel. Set on a hill in wooded grounds, this was once the haunt of the British escaping the heat of the plains and had been a favourite of the Nehru family throughout the thirties and forties. At the time we stayed there, it was already less fashionable and had lost much of its earlier glory and prestige and since this was out of season, there were also very few guests so that we tended to rattle around a bit in its large spaces.

We only stayed for five days, taking walks along shady, wooded roads or exploring the many tiny souvenir shops along the narrow central street of the town where monkeys sat on the rooftops waiting to pounce on anything that took their fancy. We visited the little cemetery where, among adult headstones, many tiny graves painted a horrific picture of just what British families in India, for all their privileges, had to sacrifice. Taking picnic lunches, we drove out along mountain roads where we saw small coolies, bent almost double under huge loads, trudging up impossible slopes and, on one of these drives, a colourful group of Tibetan refugees on their way back to their settlement called Happy Valley. It was a welcome respite before we returned to face the upheaval of moving on to a new job and possibly a new country.

We did not in the end have time to agonise over our decision. Everything happened much faster than we had anticipated. Within a month of our return, Fi had found a post with an American dairy company in Tehran and we had to begin a swift dismantling of all that we had so slowly and carefully built up together. We had taken on many responsibilities and we needed to leave everyone as well settled as possible. Ram Singh had been saving diligently all this time and decided to go back to his village and work on his family land. Fi found Mehdi, so bright and deserving, a worthwhile job in the production department of the factory. We felt that Sherry was still young enough to adapt to new people and she was taken in by our engineer's family.

In September 1966, after a formal but emotional farewell party in the factory with all the staff present and sad, private goodbyes to all our friends, we took our last journey on the Frontier Mail to Bombay and stayed there for a week before flying out to Iran.

When I married Fi and went out to India, to remote rural India, I was, like all displaced and uprooted people, setting myself two challenges – to find a new and viable identity and to find a place in the world that felt like home. I have never entirely resolved either problem.

I am Indianised enough to have lost my unadulterated Englishness but I am not an Indian. I am a Parsi wife but I am not a Parsi. Years after our marriage, when my children were older and we were living in Bombay, we were all invited to a family wedding. As we went to sit with my in-laws on the platform prepared for the religious ceremony, Fi and the children were allowed to stay but I was politely taken down into the body of the hall in order that my polluting presence should not upset the priests. It was not easy in these circumstances to forge a strong family identity. I sometimes wonder whether, if I had married a Hindu or a Moslem, I would have integrated into my adoptive family more wholeheartedly. Their religions would have been on offer, open to at least a token acceptance, and I would have seen more clearly from the start what adaptations were necessary. The social and cultural divide would have been wider and more obvious but such a family, with an unself-conscious sense of itself, might have changed and remodelled me more openly and easily. Parsis themselves suffer from something of an identity crisis, necessarily part of India but also torn between ancient Persia and the West. Their prosperity owes much to their close collaboration with the British and they have embraced many Western ways. This westernised veneer was a smoke screen that hid many of our underlying differences and gave me a slightly false sense of security. Much of what defines these people is still closely bound up with their religion and ancient history and I was always excluded from this. I grew fond of them and I lived happily with them but I was, in essence, an outsider.

It was interesting and pure chance that when we left India we were directly involved in Parsi history for we were benefiting from Fi's Zoroastrian credentials. The Shah was using Persia's past to validate a Pahlavi dynasty. Tyrannical and unpopular, he was bent on creating a myth of himself as the last of a long line of great Persian Emperors descending from Cyrus the Great and he was actively promoting the return of modern Zoroastrians. There were diplomatic differences between India and Iran at that time that made entry difficult for Indians but Fi easily got a work permit.

We stayed in Iran for two and a half years, nine months in Tehran and the remaining time in Abadan, where our son was born in a hospital that was, ironically, not a great improvement on the one I had rejected for our daughter's birth. We next went to Beirut for two years. It was at that time a peaceful and beautiful place where we enjoyed mountains and sea and world class shopping. We returned to India and lived in Bombay for ten years before going off to Indonesia, on to Yemen and finally to England. Of course these moves were dictated to an extent by the practicalities of Fi's work but I think that at some less obvious level we have always been searching for a home.

In all these places we acquired new habits and the smatterings of several new languages. Our experience of them was intense but not indelible. We have photographs and memories but no sense of their being a part of us. Bombay was rather different.

It was the first place in India that I ever saw, my in-laws had always offered it as a place of refuge, my daughter was born there and we lived there for one of the more sustained periods of our nomadic life during which time, the children had a fairly settled existence in their boarding school in Mussoorie, coming home to spend their winter holidays with us. We had also come back to Fi's original company at the invitation of the same MD with whom he had sparred over our window screens, thus reconnecting with former colleagues. My first image of India, largely shaped by life in our Northern town, the image that I have tried to project here, was for a time, coloured, even distorted, by the experience of being worn down by the city's difficult climate and by urban life taken to the extreme. On our factory site we had loved Diwali and the charm of our pretty oil lamps but in 1970s Bombay, we came to hate what had become a festival of noise rather than light, with fireworks detonated between closely packed high rise buildings making it sound as if we were living in the midst of World War Three. This level of noise, unrelenting at all times of the day and in every season, was exhausting and finally all became too much for us. We once again uprooted ourselves, though holding on to a tenuous connection with Bombay through Fi's family. Now, his brother still lives in their parents' flat in Carmichael Road, which is still one of the better areas of the city but he tells us that even higher, more gigantic tower blocks are now looming over this pleasant place.

Today, from the modernity and comfort of our current English home and the security of a relationship that has survived many years of pleasure and pain, weathering the inevitable misunderstandings and pressures that outside attitudes put upon it, I look back over that shared history which spans six countries and fifteen homes, has encompassed the birth of a daughter in one country and a son in another and involved a sustained effort to deal with the practicalities of life within the context of varied cultural norms, using many different currencies and communicating in the basics of five languages. I see how in all that time, amidst all those changes, I have never completely answered either of the two questions raised by my decision to break the rules and leave my own country. I also see that after so many changes, it is still those early years, that first experience of a foreign country, that first little town that really haunt me.

India often drove me to fury and despair. Its climate was physically debilitating, exposure to its smells, sights and sounds, its pervasive deprivations was emotionally draining and yet…. I am not the first person to have literally shaken its dust off my feet and escaped to a more congenial place only to find that, deep within, it is inescapable. In reviving these memories I am recognising a process by which this infuriating, exciting, impossible, heart-breaking country became part of the intimate fabric of my life and subtly, slowly changed the ways in which I thought and behaved.

On that day in September when we left it, I remember standing in my hard won garden looking out over the dry, dusty fields and back to the austere white block of the factory with its looming chimney. I was filled with a sense of achievement, an excited anticipation of another unknown world and a very real sadness.

Seven years earlier, I had been sitting in the courtyard of Dilkhusha wondering how I would get through my first day there, let alone all the days ahead of me. Many people had been sure that I would not make it and had uttered dire warnings about what I was doing. I had once complained to Fi that no-one had mentioned bandits but they were right not to have done so. This wasn't because I was unlikely to encounter them – though I didn't – nor because they did not exist – they did. In 1983, there was a dramatic, much publicised surrender of a female leader of a gang in Uttar Pradesh, known as the Bandit Queen who, in a weird twist, became an MP, wrote an autobiography that was made into a film and was then murdered by the family of one of her numerous former victims and as recently as 2014, another gang demanded that villagers living near their stronghold